The Conference Board

Research Report Number 949

Work and Family Policies: The New Strategic Plan

Executives and Leading Experts Discuss:

- *innovations in corporate programs*

- *creating a family supportive company culture*

- *the impact of globalization and demographics*

- *costs and benefits of work and family policies*

About The Conference Board

Founded in 1916, The Conference Board's twofold purpose is to improve the business enterprise system and to enhance the contribution of business to society.

To accomplish this, The Conference Board strives to be the leading global business membership organization that enables senior executives from all industries to explore and exchange ideas of impact on business policy and practices. To support this activity, The Conference Board provides a variety of forums and a professionally managed research program that identifies and reports objectively on key areas of changing management concern, opportunity and action.

The Conference Board
845 Third Avenue
New York, NY 10022-6601
Telephone 212 759-0900
Fax 212 980-7014

The Conference Board Europe
Avenue Louise
207 - Bte 5, B-1050
Brussels, Belgium
Telephone 02 640 6240
Fax 02 640 6735

The Conference Board of Canada
255 Smyth Road
Ottawa, Ontario, KIH-8M7
Telephone 613 526-3280
Fax 613 926-4857

Work and Family Policies: The New Strategic Plan

Edited by James L. Peters
          Barbara H. Peters
          and Frank Caropreso

Contents

From the President

An overflow audience at The Conference Board's Work and Family Conference this year proved to be a strong testament to the fresh urgency and concern for work-family issues in the business community. Time and again company representatives at the conference proved eager to explore innovative ways to attract and retain a talented workforce. Paid leave for family illness, parental leave plus elder care benefits — all major concerns for today's worker — are now appearing at the top of the corporate agenda. Reshaping the corporate environment to make it more family-friendly is not seen as a "good work," but rather as a sound strategy for doing good business.

The presentations in this volume are the highlights from that conference. On behalf of the Board, I would like to thank the speakers and attendees for making this conference such a resounding success.

PRESTON TOWNLEY
President and CEO

Introduction

Dana E. Friedman
Co-Founder and Co-President
Families and Work Institute
Conference Chair

I coordinated The Conference Board's first conference on work and family in 1986. Looking back at the agenda, one can see how far this issue has come. Most of that one-day event was spent reviewing demographics and making the case for work and family as a legitimate business issue. At this conference, we will again discuss the rationale for corporate involvement, but most of the time will be spent exploring how to implement effective programs and policies.

Significant changes have occurred in recent years. In 1986 there were about 2,500 companies providing child care support; today there are about 5,400. Elder care was a footnote at the 1986 conference; today there are more than 300 companies offering a wide array of elder care benefits.

Until recently, corporate people who were sympathetic to the work-family movement were quiet about their commitment, lest they be seen as radicals. But increasingly work-family champions see their advocacy of work-family issues as a stepping stone to more credibility within their companies, more contact with the CEO and more visibility in the public arena.

A final distinction is that during the 1980s, we expected employees to do most of the accommodating—whether it was redefining their own relationships, working out new arrangements with community services, or revising their career expectations. In the 1990s, changes will occur in organizations. They will not only look at work-family issues but they will try to connect them to other strategic concerns. Most important, organizations will need to examine basic principles—perhaps how we view work itself.

We are here today to explore and encourage this process.

The Future Is Not What It Was, And Why Companies Care

[Preston Townley, President and Chief Executive Officer, The Conference Board, interviewed William S. Lee and Reuben Mark after they made introductory remarks.]

William S. Lee
Chairman and President
Duke Power Company

Duke Power serves 1.5 million homes in the two Carolinas with a team of 19,000 people. Our interest in family issues directly relates to the bottom line. Family issues in the workplace impact productivity and affect our ability to attract and retain highly capable people. This, as well as our compassion, drives our interest in the family.

The one word that characterizes our human resources policy is flexibility. In the last year, for example, we have discarded about half our human resources procedures. More and more we trust management, supervisors and employees throughout the organization to make HR decisions without the book. We think this approach best serves the workplace of the future. We have been through an era of affirmative action. We are now mature enough to trust one another not to discriminate, and we don't need complicated procedural manuals. Flexibility increasingly permeates our organization and provides more freedom to decide at the local level.

Reuben Mark
President and Chief Executive Officer
Colgate-Palmolive Company

Colgate-Palmolive is a global company. Two-thirds of our $5 billion revenue comes from outside the United States. We have operations in 60 countries and sell products in 160 nations. Most of Colgate's management are either foreign-born or have spent a good deal of their careers overseas. This is important for the cor-

porate culture because these executives have firsthand experience with the value of cultural and ethnic diversity.

At the beginning of the last decade, we started an eight-year plan to revitalize the company. The objectives were to focus the company and increase shareholder value and profitability. The mechanism to do this was largely people-oriented: increase motivation, push decision making down, empower employees. We cut out management levels, divested 40 companies, and reconfigured factories.

Human resources played an important role in the development of this plan. The most profound changes were in HR. For the first time, we recruited top-flight professionals to do the job. And they helped us change our culture. First we completed a conversion to pay-for-performance in our business. But we also did many things to make the 27,000 employees—downsized from about 50,000—know that they were contributing significantly to the company's success. This approach centered on human issues and drove us into the work-family sphere.

Developing a family-friendly workplace is the right thing to do and must be done from both a social and moral viewpoint. Beyond this, it is good business and one of the mechanisms needed to attract, motivate and retain quality people. The best decision maker in this area is the individual employee. Over the next decade, Colgate will focus on work-family issues. Unless company leadership deals with this daily and emphasizes it in words and policies, it won't happen. It must be led from the top.

Townley: You cite the bottom line as a strong reason for pursuing action in this area. Is there a single fact or concept that brings this home?

Lee: Today management's role is to create an opportunity for employees to become excited about their contribution to the workplace. You can't get excited about your work if you are worried about a sick child at home. So the sick child at home is a concern to management. We want to do something about this issue specifically and many other family-related issues.

Mark: This is one element of an overall view that the way a business remains successful is by developing employees who are motivated, loyal and satisfied with the work they are doing.

Townley: There are critics who view some of this activity as a response to external social concerns rather than the bottom line. Would you comment?

Lee: These concerns are motivated by the bottom line. I don't think we should undertake a social program that is somehow not connected to the bottom line. Our obligation to our customers and shareholders and employees is that we be a competitive, profitable enterprise.

Mark: I think we diverge a bit here. In a democratic society, all institutions—in addition to their primary responsibilities—have an obligation to put their efforts to socially appropriate activity. Colgate, for example, is deeply involved in education in New York City, because we have focused our non-profit work as we have focused our business. We would be hard-pressed to find a direct link to the bottom line as a result of this focus on New York's education. But we are residents and enjoy the benefits of New York. From the perspective of a social contract, we must pay something back.

Lee: I see a direct connection between the quality of education in New York City and the success of Colgate here. Your employees live here; the quality of life is affected by the quality of education; therefore the success of your company is affected by it. I see a direct connection to our future bottom line in the Carolinas and the quality of education in the territory we serve.

Mark: In addition to my belief that it is the right thing to do, there is no doubt that it is the mission of management to get the most dedicated, loyal, motivated workforce possible to embrace the company's vision.

Clearly this is one of the important mechanisms to achieve this mission. Without it, you will not reach the bottom line.

Townley: How do you measure the bottom line and the P&L impact? Or do you?

Lee: An example of a family issue that relates to our bottom line is that we have 500 alcoholics on payroll. They are sober. About an equal number of employee family members have an alcohol problem. And they are sober. Through our employee assistance program, we have worked to rehabilitate a population of about 1,000. I know how many counselors we have and what our annual budget is for the program.

We include treatment for alcoholism as part of our medical expense. Those 500 employees have 5,000 years of experience. If we had not rehabilitated them, we would have had to recruit 500 new employees, train them, and build up an equivalent 5,000 years of experience. You can imagine the cost of recruiting and training 500 employees. The cost of our employee assistance program has been returned to us many times. It is improving the bottom line.

Mark: You don't need specific cost justification for this. The first course in psychology tells you the effect of employees' problems on their productivity. If we can reduce external pressures and improve the way people think about themselves, productivity will increase. You can construct a huge research project to divine the savings or incremental profits here, but we know the answer going in: if you are motivated, you do better. Work-family flexibility is one of the mechanisms to motivate.

Townley: Even though a CEO supports the work and family concept, how do you deal with the senior manager who is running a profitable division despite the fact he or she is only paying lip service to work-family issues?

Mark: It is the role of the CEO to set a company's strategic vision, get the right people in the right jobs and then make sure they are motivated. The things we are talking about today are integral to that process.

So this becomes one of the most difficult jobs—to push top-level commitment down through the organization. Managers must be reminded, sometimes heavy handedly, that they are being evaluated on three criteria: volume, profit and meeting company objectives. At the end of the year, they will be rated in terms of meeting objectives such as work-family. You must use this kind of evaluation tool and use it hard.

Lee: I agree. If you use performance-based pay and encounter a senior manager whose feet are in concrete, you can establish a performance goal in the area of weakness. The manager will understand this. Performance-based pay can help achieve many goals.

Townley: What kind of support do you expect or get from your human resources function?

Mark: The integration of human resources into the management function is a vital component of Colgate's strategy. It is a two-way partnership. I am here today because human resources knew this would be an important forum and that it would be a way to further influence our management group. If I feel strongly about being here, managers will take note.

Lee: Our human resources department has helped drive a cultural change at Duke Power toward greater flexibility. And I am here because of their urging.

Townley: A so-called "mandated benefits debate" exists in Washington and among certain business groups. What are your views on the role of government in these kinds of issues?

Lee: Government social programs have been a driving force in this country. We wouldn't have come this far in non-discrimination were it not for government impetus. At the same time, we have government programs that are highly structured, restrictive and overly complicated. This hampers the flexibility that is often the key to success in human resources matters. I tend to prefer fewer government programs and more freedom to initiate.

Mark: I agree in principle. But if we are to spread these practices throughout the country broadly and deeply, inevitably government pressures will be necessary. The civil rights legislation of the 1960s was critical to that movement. Similar legislation in the work-family area is required. Operating in many foreign countries, we at Colgate find that you can always count on certain nations to make things happen. The job before us is to get the bottom half of companies up to standard. To do this, there must be pressure.

The Diversity of Work-Family Issues

[Judy Woodruff, Chief Washington Correspondent for the MacNeil/Lehrer Newshour, introduced a panel of employees representing different generations and family models. They presented brief profiles of themselves and answered questions from Ms. Woodruff and the audience. Their profiles and selected responses follow.]

David S. Machlowitz
Assistant General Counsel
General Instrument Corp.

At work, I am involved in environmental, employment and product liability law. At home, I am the father of a two-year-old daughter. My wife works full-time. I left private practice and entered the corporate world, in part, to get more control over my life so that I could spend more time with my family. Our daughter is cared for by someone who comes to our home for the day. It still leaves us subject to the 6:00 a.m. or even the 2:00 a.m. call when the babysitter has a crisis in her own life. Then we have to decide who can take the morning off and who can take the afternoon off or who can take the baby to the office and for how long.

Young children need quantity time. From my perspective, the notion that quality time is enough is not valid. My wife and I have made sacrifices in our careers so that we can spend more time with our daughter. We both work more predictable schedules now.

The downside of professional life is that the obligations can be extreme. When I punch out, the obligations come with me. Many friends tell me that their companies are not receptive to the idea of fathers who want to take time off to go to the school appointed pediatrician. The "that's women's work" attitude persists. Viewpoints are beginning to change slowly. We have already seen, for example, husbands who will not relocate without considering how it will impact their wives' career.

Claire Lifshitz,
Office Manager
OCAW Local 8149

I am married, my husband works full-time, and I have four children. I have one at home full-time, the others I share with their colleges. I best represent your blue-collar worker—the production worker on the assembly line or most of your clerical staff. Working full-time with children creates continual problems. For people who work in factories and lower-level office jobs, financial flexibility usually isn't available. Companies therefore must provide work flexibility and understanding.

When you punch a time clock, your children don't exist. You don't go to the supervisor and tell him that you must go home to care for a sick or injured child. You punch out in the face of many complaints; you will not be paid for the time; and if you do this too often, you will be looking for another job. Things are changing slowly. But when you get down into most companies' production lines, the script still says, "If you want to work, be here and you will get paid."

If you work in a factory and it has put your children in the attic, why would you expect your elders to be treated any better? I worked with a woman who was fired for taking time off to care for a semi-senile mother; she was the only person who was available to care for her mother. The company's attitude was that the mother was an adult and didn't require the daughter's help. This is an irresponsible position.

People who are distracted are not good employees. If they are worried about elderly parents or sick children, they are not giving you their best work. And replacing them means hiring untrained employees. Each time a trained person walks out the door you lose her or his technique and speed: You lose production.

Robyn Person
Assistant in Human Resources
Home Box Office

I am in charge of the in-house temporary employment program at HBO. I am the single mother of a 17-month-old daughter who is asthmatic. It is important that I work for a company that is flexible about dependent care needs. Before my employment at HBO, it was very difficult for me. I had to be at home with my daughter a lot; I worried about her when I was at work; I felt guilty about my work and my child.

HBO has an emergency child care service. If my daughter is too sick to go to the babysitter's, if she is mildly ill, the service sends someone to my home to care for her—at the company's expense. It is a wonderful benefit. If my former employer could see me now—without the child care stress—if they could see my performance at HBO, they would know that this kind of benefit makes a world of difference.

Henry Baird
Researcher
AT&T Bell Labs

I carry out basic research in computer science. I represent a wide variety of non-traditional family relationships, those not defined by blood, marriage or adoption. For the last eight years I have lived with Clark Mazuick, my domestic partner. Our family includes my elderly parents whom we are helping through their final illnesses and related difficulties. I also help Clark raise his 11-year-old child from a former marriage. He doesn't benefit from AT&T's generous survivor pension annuities, health plan and other important benefits. We have had to strain with an extraordinary rate of pre-tax savings in order to prepare for the possibility that I should die before he does.

An essential component to being comfortable about claiming benefits is feeling free to explain your family relationship to your bosses. Many families know that their particular circumstances aren't recognized—not by their bosses and not by the formal company policies. About 10 percent of your employees are gay or lesbian. Yet we are in the earliest stages of these employees stepping forward, identifying themselves, explaining their particular arrangements and asking for the benefits that their circumstances require. In the future, employers will meet many more people from the lesbian and gay population who are prepared to do this.

When my mother had a serious stroke and my parents' home became untenable, I had to move them to an apartment near me in New Jersey. We virtually set up a small nursing home there. My work productivity declined 25 percent. Fortunately there was time flexibility at work, and I have a computer terminal at home. But there was tremendous pressure.

Betty Hudson
Senior Vice President
Corporate Communications, NBC, Inc.

I am 41-years-old and the mother of a 2.5-year-old and a five-month-old. At work I supervise a staff of 130. We have had eight babies born within our division in the last year and one child was adopted. My husband is a television correspondent whose show was canceled in January. We have live-in child care. I recognize that I am in a privileged situation because I have the resources to make child care in my home a reality. But I don't have a blood relative within 2000 miles of New York. So we are dealing with the issue of what a nuclear family really means.

My job is being the company's chief spokesperson. The company is helpful: I have fax machines and company phone lines at home. But if I have to look at the whole landscape of what my family responsibilities are—including running the house—it is daunting, especially if I look at it as a 20-year issue. I must look at it in small bites.

To a certain extent, what is going on in the lives of the people who are the company's policy makers drives much of the corporate attitude. The message from the top may be subtle but it ripples out to the troops, and this can mean positive change.

NBC is coming into an increased consciousness about work-family issues. But we need supervisors who are able to talk more openly and honestly with employees when they sense family-related problems. Things are slowly changing.

Innovative but Replicable—Corporate Responses to Family Needs

CHILD CARE

Rosemary Mans

Vice President and Manager, Work-Family Programs, Bank of America

In the last decade many companies responded to work-family issues. Today, about 5400 major U.S. employers offer some form of child care. The most popular choices are:

(1) Dependent care assistance programs. About 2,500 companies have selected this option and it is by far the most common response. It allows pre-tax salary deductions for employees who set aside dollars for dependent care.

(2) Resource and referral assistance. About 1,200 companies try to help their employees find quality child care through R&R programs.

(3) Child care centers near or on-site. About 1,200 employers provide this option: 800 hospitals, 200 non-hospital corporations and 200 government agencies.

(4) Specialized forms of financing, such as vouchers or discount arrangements. This factors in affordability for employees. About 100 companies offer this assistance.

(5) Other responses, in about 100 companies, include family day care strategies in communities near the company; after-school programs for latchkey children; and sick child care assistance.

Future Trends

In the future, you can expect companies that now have some form of child care assistance to offer a variety of options. Companies with multiple locations will expand from one pilot site to other locations. One important trend is that companies are starting to use resource and referral agencies more imaginatively. Resource and referral agencies are the source for multiple kinds of child care responses. They can, for example, manage voucher programs or share their expertise in workplace seminars. These agencies can be much more than the source of referrals.

Increasingly, companies acknowledge the sick child care issue and are working toward a solution. We have already seen efforts to develop external services to respond to this need. One is the provision of in-home caregivers—an expensive but effective alternative. We will also see growth in corporate flexibility toward sick child care leave time, whether it is allowing employees to use their own sick days or some combination of emergency or personal time off. About 60 percent of major corporations are experimenting with the time off issue but over half are doing it on an unpaid basis. Unpaid versus paid time off is a critical question, especially for lower level employees.

There will be more growth in dependent care assistance plans although companies are beginning to see limitations here. The lower level employees, those making under $25,000, do not benefit as much using a dependent care assistance plan as they might from a tax credit.

We are starting to see more collaboration between companies to build a stable supply of care. After all, resource and referral can only be effective when there is something we can refer people to. Companies can pool resources to expand supply. This is what the California Child Care Initiative is all about. Some companies are now developing their own funds to help community-based organizations create more care.

J.T. Childs, Jr.
Manager, Work/Life Programs
IBM Corporation

IBM's child care initiative emerged in 1984. We announced a national child care referral service to be managed for us by Work/Family Directions. We didn't take this step in response to a ground swell of expressed employee concern. Rather, we moved in this direction because demographic data told us that this was where business leaders must move if they are to be responsive to employees' needs. Our employees had yet to see child care as an issue that required their company's involvement. They thought of child care as a family matter and that they should manage it.

In 1986 we distributed a random work/life survey to 4,000 people at IBM. Seventy-eight percent responded. And we learned many interesting things about these IBM employees. We already knew that the population was about 70 percent male. Projecting from 1965 to 2000, however, our male population will decline 25 percent and the female population will triple. We will be between 36-38 percent female by the year 2000. This fact alone prompts a strong business interest in family issues.

We learned that 58 percent of our employees were members of a dual-income family. About 30 percent reported they had children who required supervision. Among people under 40 years of age, 55 percent of the dual-professional families and 38 percent of the dual-earners said they planned to have or adopt a child within the next five years.

We asked employees if they had missed a day of work during the past year due to an ill child at home. And 60 percent said they had missed at least one day while 30 percent said they had missed three or more days. We converted this to a productivity hit of $30 million based on the lost productivity. We thought this factor alone justified the development of our program for mildly ill children.

Child Care Objective

Our child care objective is simply stated: to assist our employees regardless of their location, income, children's ages, or the type of care required. We hoped to address the full range of family needs. These needs were defined as:
- Finding care

- Knowing how to select among the various options
- Finding care consistent with the ability to pay
- Identifying care options that don't currently exist

IBM has one contract with Work/Family Directions and they have 250 local contracts. Wherever our employees live, they have access to a local resource and referral agency. IBM decided not to initiate on-site child care. We don't know how to do it equitably. Our plan is to focus on resource and referral and supply; to maximize parental choice; and to deliver the service consistently and equitably. The five-year results are impressive. We have served 39,000 families and 45,000 children through the service. Of the children, 70 percent are under three-years-old and 40 percent are under age one.

Dependent Care Initiative

In November 1989, we announced the IBM Funds for Dependent Care Initiatives- -$25 million over five years—$22 million for child care, $3 million for elder care. When we considered this investment, we focused on communities where IBM had significant populations.

The initiative's focus will include day care centers, family day care recruitment; programs for school-aged children; and programs for mildly ill children. Prior to this initiative, IBM had not aggressively addressed the subject of day care centers. Our investment in day care centers will aim at securing limited priority enrollment for the children of IBM parents. Regarding programs for mildly ill children, we want to provide alternatives for parents when a child is ill. Of course, we want employees to come to work. But we have emphasized to managers that the decision to come to work or not when a child is ill should be made by the parent. We don't want managers inhibiting this process.

Flexibility for Caregivers

A series of flexibility measures was announced at IBM in 1988. We increased personal leave from one to three years. During a three-year leave, full benefits remain in effect. In the second and third years, you must be available for part-time work, up to 20 hours a week. Before this policy went into effect, about 2,000 employees were on leave at any given time; now about 2,500 are on leave. We have noted a small number of men taking leaves in conjunction with the birth of children.

A work-at-home pilot is underway in 10 locations. We aren't migrating work to the home. Rather this is designed for employees on personal leave who cannot come to the workplace. Participants must perform the type of work that can be accomplished at home and must report to their regular work for four consecutive hours each week. If the job requires a computer terminal, IBM will install one in the home. We think this may be an attractive and manageable alternative, especially for those with caregiving responsibilities.

We also expanded our individualized work schedules to a two-hour window. If your work day normally runs 8:30 to 4:30, you can now begin as early as 7:30 or as late as 9:30 and end at 3:30 or 5:30. At two pilot sites, we have a mid-day flex. This allows employees to add up to two hours to their lunch hour. You must make this time up in the same calendar day. An employee on the second shift told us that her baby normally went to bed at the time of her lunch hour. With mid-day flex, she can now go home and help put her baby to bed.

In 1989 IBM implemented a management development module that all 30,000 U.S. managers will participate in. The module builds the business case for work/life programs. IBM wants to make it clear that we are implementing work/life programs to help employees balance work demands and family pressures. We will still demand excellence but the work will be done differently. The varied programs are tools for managers to use in building partnerships with their employees so that IBM can remain a globally competitive company.

Sandra M. Colley
Director, E.E.O.
John Hancock Mutual Life Insurance Company

At John Hancock we began looking at family care in the traditional way—with a task force. Our goal was to define employees' family care needs and the appropriate employer response to those needs. In our research we attended seminars, made on-site visits to child care centers, surveyed other employers, interviewed John Hancock managers, surveyed our employees and consulted with leading work-family experts. We struggled with these issues for many months, recognizing that there wasn't one solution for all employees.

Corporate Family Care Policy

Our initiatives included a statement on family care that is part of our corporate policy guide. It says:

"The John Hancock believes its employees are one of its greatest strengths. In recent years, the life style and needs of our employees have been changing. The increase in dual wage earners and working parents in our workforce is a trend that we believe will continue into the future and represents a portion of our workforce that is vital to our continued success as a corporation. Recognizing that employees have responsibilities to their families as well as to their jobs, the John Hancock will endeavor to provide an environment and policies that

are supportive to our employees' achieving their own necessary balance between work and family issues."

To assist our managers and supervisors in the day-to-day operation of the programs, we have expanded managerial training to include family care sensitivity training. We want to help managers be more supportive in dealing with employees and family care issues. We have also created a human resources staff position to be an advocate for family care issues and to do ongoing research on family care.

John Hancock recognizes that employees need flexibility when they are caring for others. We therefore implemented three enhancements to our time and leave policies:

(1) Employees may use up to three of their available sick days for an illness in the family.

(2) Flextime hours have been expanded so that employees may better balance child or elder care needs.

(3) Unpaid leave of absence has been extended to a maximum of one year with full company benefits.

Family policies include a benefit that allows employees to call home to check on family members. For those people who don't normally have access to a work phone, one call home to a latchkey child provides great relief and a more productive employee. A flexible spending account has also been established that allows pre-tax dollars to pay for child or elder care expenses. An adoption benefit provides 100 percent reimbursement for the first $2,000 of related expenses. And John Hancock's child care referral service operates throughout Massachusetts, providing employees with information on child care providers in their communities.

Child Care Initiatives

An exciting new initiative is called Kids to Go. This is an effort to provide child care during school holidays and vacations when the company is open. Frequently employees take vacation time to cover the home front in these periods. Kids to Go, a collaboration between John Hancock and Ellis Memorial, a non-profit Boston child care agency, provides activities for employees' children, ages six to thirteen, during specified holidays and vacation weeks. Parents can bring their children to the company as early as 7:30 a.m. and pick them up by 4:30 p.m. Ellis Memorial groups the children by age and schedules movies, museum visits, bowling, roller skating and other activities. Over 70 children attended our first week-long program in February and it was a great success.

Another new program is Summer Care Fair, a trade fair, where information about summer programs is made available to employees. The fair is a way for many summer camp managers and programmers to be available for employees—all under John Hancock's roof.

John Hancock's most exciting family care initiative is the development of an on-site child care center beginning later this year. Employees have responded enthusiastically to this announcement. Initially the center will serve 100 children and then increase to a capacity of 200.

Though each of us may not share the responsibility of child care, we work daily with people who do. We want to work with the best qualified and most productive people. To the extent that we can put policies and programs in place that help our employees be more productive, we are all winners.

Elder Care

Angela Heath
Program Specialist
American Association for Retired Persons

AARP and the Travelers Company Foundation conducted a national survey of caregivers in 1988. They found that seven million households face elder care issues. Most pertinent, perhaps, they reported that 55 percent of the caregivers work outside the home. The New York Business Group on Health completed research earlier, in 1985, that revealed how corporate decision makers viewed elder care and its effects on their companies. The consensus was that elder care problems led to decreased productivity, overuse of company telephones for personal needs, and increased absenteeism.

Corporate response to elder care is a recent phenomenon. Pioneers in the mid-1980s included Travelers with its landmark research; the University of Bridgeport, which looked at different kinds of supports for Pepsico, Remington Steel and People's Bank; and Aerospace Corporation in California which developed work and family clubs.

Since the mid-80s, hundreds of U.S. companies have begun implementing elder care programs: Pepsico and other firms set up an elder care hotline in the Connecticut area; Champion International developed literature on elder care issues; American Express and Hallmark Cards offer educational seminars in the workplace; IBM and Johnson & Johnson signed referral and consultation contracts; and AT&T provides seed money to communities to develop caregiver supports.

It is said that elder care may be the benefit issue of the 1990s. In a rapidly aging world, elder issues do hold out the promise to revolutionize work and family policies.

Donald E. Hillier
Assistant Vice President, Corporate Human
Resources
Aetna Life and Casualty

Aetna began its elder care services in September 1988 in conjunction with its child care initiatives. We didn't conduct an employee survey or spend an extraordinary amount of time studying this issue. We reviewed a number of other companies' studies, discussed alternative services with providers and other companies, and decided to add elder care services to balance our child care initiatives and thus appeal to a greater number of employees.

Aetna's elder care service includes three major parts:
- Consultation and referral
- Work time seminars
- Support groups

Consultation and Referral Network

The goals of our consultation and referral service are: (1) to help employees understand the community and state care options; (2) to help employees find services they need; (3) to provide employees and their families with literature to better deal with elder issues and make informed decisions; (4) and to provide ongoing emotional support during and after the search for services. Employees may call as frequently as they wish for support or to discuss issues as they arise.

Aetna has contracted with Work/Family Directions to deliver this service. Work/Family has identified hundreds of agencies across the U.S. that are experts in elder care services. These local community-based agencies actually provide the services to our employees. To access these services, employees call a toll-free number in the location where the elder resides or needs service. After consultation, local referrals are made and appropriate reading materials are provided to assist the employee.

Local elder care agencies also develop additional community services as part of their contracts with Aetna and other companies. The agencies identify areas of shortage, and corporations jointly fund the development of services to fill the gaps. About 10 percent of our annual fee to Work/Family Directions is earmarked for this development of services.

Elder care topics are one component of Aetna's seminar program. Employee seminars are free and held during the work day for two-and-a-half hours. We frequently repeat a topic several times to meet a large demand. We also offer employee support groups that meet during lunch hours for eight weeks. A professional social worker leads the support group. One group expressed a need to continue the support after eight weeks, and they now meet monthly on their own time.

At Aetna we have learned that employees aren't as assertive about elder care issues as they are about child care needs. Few employees, however, know how to identify and locate the services they may need. People feel they should be able to handle their aging parents or "significant others." It is a very emotional issue. In addition, there is a real concern about privacy.

Most important, we know that by being flexible and supportive with families, Aetna gains an advantage in attracting and retaining a loyal and productive workforce in today's tight labor market.

Karen Leibold
Director, Work and Family Programs
Stride Rite Children's Centers

Stride Rite's 20-year vision and commitment to child care led us quite naturally to thinking about elder care. The corporate elder care movement has grown rapidly—partly because most decision makers have aging parents and few of them have young children anymore. Other well known factors are: the over-85 population is the fastest growing segment in our society; women, who are the traditional caregivers have gone to work; and the workforce is shrinking and aging.

Stride Rite's response to the elder care crisis is multi-faceted. We have resource and referral for elder care; several free series of lunchtime seminars; and on-site, individual counseling for employees with elder caregiving responsibilities.

Intergenerational Day Care Center

The most innovative thing we have done is expand one of our on-site child care facilities to include adult day care. It is now the Intergenerational Day Care Center. We have worked on this project for three years and the center just opened in February. Stride Rite gave us 8,500 square feet of space in our corporate headquarters in Cambridge, which was renovated into a new intergenerational center. Our capacity is 55 children, age 15 months through kindergarten, and 24 elders over 60 in need of adult day care.

Our initiative has three major goals:

(1) To provide the service for employees and families who live or work in the community. About half the spaces in our centers have always been reserved for community people; we have continued this with the elder program. Some people are from low-income families and the state subsidizes their care.

(2) To produce a replicable model. Stride Rite is creating an intergenerational model. We don't see many programs today mixing the very young and very old.

We are also creating a model for employer sponsorship, and public/private collaborations.

(3) To create baseline research on what happens to children and elders in this kind of care setting and what happens to the workplace and the community.

This idea came from Stride Rite's chairman. He read a Wall Street Journal article about a New York City family who had a young child and an elderly mother living with them. We spent one year determining whether it made sense to bring the two generations together and whether there was a need for a corporate response to elder care. In the second year, we did an employee needs assessment and found that one-fourth of our employees had elder care responsibilities. An additional 13 percent expected to assume such care in the next five years. This matches the national average. In the third year, we got into the nuts and bolts of the project—budget, program, space.

Adult day care is relatively new and we must educate people about what it is and who it is for. These are not surrogate grandparents for the children. Rather they are people who require care for themselves during the day. However, the children and elders at the Stride Rite Center are enjoying each other already.

We thought it would be wise to bring them together slowly with many staff-directed activities; we thought relationships would take some time to develop. But because the press wanted pictures of the two groups together, we staged a photo session that lasted over an hour, and we learned that the two groups truly do enjoy each other. We were perhaps being too conservative about the issue. In the years ahead, we hope you will be hearing a great deal about the remarkable success we all believe this Intergenerational Center will be.

Alternative Work Schedules

Kathleen E. Christensen
Director
National Project on Home-Based Work

We have come a long way in a short time. There is no better example than alternative work schedules—those schedules that vary from the routine 9-5, Monday-Friday, 12-month-a-year job. In 1984 I surveyed 7,000 American women who worked at home, almost 80 percent of them self-employed. When asked why they were self-employed, the nearly universal response—if they had children—was to better balance work and family. They all reported trying to set up alternative schedules when they had their first child.

Because of the lack of workplace alternatives through the mid-1980s, many women quit the corporate world and built their own businesses. This represented a great loss to U.S. corporations since they had invested heavily in the women, and the women had gained considerable experience and skills. By the late 1980s, we see a different scenario. American companies realize that alternative schedules are a good way to do business, that there are bottom-line interests to be served by providing alternatives.

Scheduling: Options and Progress

Recently, I finished a report, Flexible Staffing and Scheduling in U.S. Corporations, for The Conference Board in which I reported that companies have made real progress in this area. In a survey of 521 of the largest U.S. corporations, we found that over 90 percent of the firms were providing some kind of alternative schedule. The most common type of arrangement was part-time work and the second most popular was flextime. Almost one-fifth of the firms offered job sharing; about 7 percent offered work at home. Over one-third of the companies granted compressed work weeks—a 40-hour work week worked in less than five days.

Many companies implemented compressed work weeks for the traditional reason—production needs. Others, however, increasingly used this schedule as an alternative scheduling strategy for work-family needs. Companies report anticipated growth in their use of flexible schedules in the coming years. Many are considering job sharing. Flextime and work at home—telecommuting—are other arrangements where they see future growth. In the last six years, I have seen real growth in the number of companies either implementing work at home in privately negotiated deals or beginning to explore company-wide work-at-home policies.

Challenges remain for implementing and managing alternative schedules. They include:

(1) A need to manage the program optimally—by objectives and bottom-line interests; satisfaction with the ease of supervision is not high.

(2) A need to create a culture in which men feel free to choose flexible schedules; with the exception of telecommuting, women preponderantly choose alternative arrangements.

(3) A need to expand schedule options beyond the clerical ranks; alternatives are mainly pursued by clerical administrative support or sales personnel.

(4) A need to expand usage of these options within companies; relatively few employees pursue alternative options.

Deborah L. Holt

Manager, Human Resources Policies and Programs
US Sprint/United Communications Company

US Sprint is 3.5-years-old, and in that time, less than half of one percent of its 16,000 member workforce has left due to family-related issues. Sprint has also had no problem with recruitment, boasting instead steady staff growth of 15 percent per year. Why would an infant company like Sprint, which hasn't experienced turnover, recruitment or productivity problems, invest heavily in family support programs to meet future workforce needs? Because we know it makes good business sense.

After we assessed Sprint's employee needs, we designed our comprehensive Family Care program. It offers multiple-support resources, such as workplace flexibility, to help employees manage career and family needs. Through employee-involvement groups, action-planning teams and individual interviews, we developed the program's blueprint. It is designed to help every employee—regardless of level—resolve family-related issues. And we did this in just five months.

Flexibility Measures

Sprint's workplace flexibility program, an important component of the Family Care initiatives, allows for schedule flexibility that meets the needs of both the business and the employee. This component grew out of alternative work schedules already in place at Sprint. By participating as task force members, management endorsed flexibility development efforts.

In general, any alternative schedule that meets both business and individual needs is encouraged. However, four basic arrangements have been designed. About 35 percent of our workforce uses some form of alternative scheduling now, and this figure is expected to continue to rise throughout the year.

(1) Flexible schedules allow employees to vary arrival, departure and lunch times under a flextour or flextime schedule. About 40 percent of all departments companywide have designed alternative schedules to satisfy business needs and employee accommodation.

(2) Compressed schedules allow employees to work longer daily hours, to a maximum of 12-hour days, to achieve a shorter work week. A popular version of compressed time is Friday half-days to extend weekends. Almost 20 percent of the workforce uses compressed schedules, and this figure is expected to grow within the year.

(3) Regular part-time and job sharing are schedules in which employees work between 20 and 40 hours a week. Applicable company benefits are pro-rated accordingly. About 5 percent of our workforce is part-time and this includes professional exempt employees. Growth in job sharing is expected in departments where multiple job incumbents and larger female populations exist. Local human resources units assist with job sharing arrangements.

(4) Flexday is designed to provide non-exempt employees with flexibility and pay to handle family-related emergencies. Throughout the year, two or more hours may be taken on short notice, to a maximum of one regularly scheduled day, to deal with family issues.

The flexibility program establishes guidelines and accountabilities, not rigid rules. This contributes to the program's success. Departments are able to pursue non-traditional scheduling as long as it makes sense for their business units. Managers and employees together assess options on a case-by-case basis. The only management requirement is to demonstrate flexibility and sensitivity to individual needs.

Michael E. Brown
Director Employee Relations
Northeast Utilities Service Company

During the early 1980s, Northeast Utilities began to receive an increasing number of employee inquiries about alternative ways to schedule work. We received requests for job sharing, part-time, flexible daily schedules and compressed work weeks. We decided that we had to develop options to meet the needs of a changing workforce.

To get started, we formed a project team from the human resources group and we consulted with an outside agency—Family and Career Together—about job sharing. The task force developed preliminary guidelines for a job sharing program and communicated the guidelines through supervisors to identify interested employees.

Job Sharing Teams

We identified 32 people who wanted to job share; so we established 16 teams to be part of a one-year pilot program from September, 1984 to September, 1985. We matched teams for the best fit. We surveyed job sharers and their supervisors to assess attitudes about the job sharing pilot. The response to the program was very favorable. We obtained final management approval and officially launched the program on December 1, 1986.

We limit job sharing to non-union employees, of which there are about 6,000. Supervisors are not included. The program requires the development of a job sharing agreement signed by the job sharers and the supervisor. We use a full-time equivalency ratio to determine vacation, sick pay, or any benefits linked to length of service. We prohibited personal time off, believing that job sharers had adequate time to manage such matters. This has proven to be a fair judgment. We provide health coverage for the job sharer only; however, insurance is available for purchase by the employee for family dependents.

We use a 50-question, true-false, self-scoring document to determine whether an employee has the flexibility, organizational, communication and collaborative skills needed to be an effective job sharer. Employees also receive a worksheet before they make the final decision to job share. They must look at the financial realities and decide if they can afford it.

At last count, we had 108 job sharers or 54 teams. The largest number by far, 80 percent, share for child care reasons; 10 percent for elder care; 5 percent for education; and 5 percent for the need or desire to work a reduced schedule. Among the 108 are 100 women and 8 men. Their ages range from those in their 20s to people in their 50s. Most people share a full five days, working half-days. Others work 2.5 days a week. Among the participants in job sharing are accountants, analysts, buyers, cashiers, clerks, computer scientists, engineers, secretaries, technicians, and text processors.

Cost vs. Benefits

Our experience is that the only additional cost is the increase in federal and state unemployment insurance taxes. Now we must pay for two employees instead of one. When we added it up, we found it cost $200 more per team in unemployment insurance taxes which is offset by the increases in productivity. In addition, we see marked reductions in the following areas: absenteeism rates compared to full-time people; the need for vendor labor, because job sharers cover for each other during vacations and illness; the turnover rate; and the work error rate, because job sharers tend to supervise each other and pick up mistakes. They generally compensate for each other's skill deficiencies as well. We have found that we have come close to 100 percent productivity through job sharing, and supervisors agree that job sharers are probably more productive than one person working a full day.

To start a program, it is key to find supportive supervisors. Try pilot programs. Be flexible. If one schedule doesn't work, rethink it. Make sure that supervisors communicate with both job sharers. If this is a problem, get the three together to figure out some way to communicate. To succeed, you must nurture these programs and continually fine tune them.

Time Off

Michele R. Lord
Senior Research Associate
Families and Work Institute

Time off includes maternity, parental and family leave as well as time off policies that don't fall under the leave umbrella—such as alternate work schedules. During the 1950s and 1960s, when people referred to leave, they were talking about leave for mothers' maternity leave. Several assumptions were made by employees at that time. There was an expectation that most women wouldn't work late into their pregnancies. Many professions, in fact, asked women to leave the workforce after the fourth or fifth month of pregnancy. And women were not expected to return from maternity leave because the traditional one-earner family was the norm. There were few families headed up by single women. If women returned to work, they did so in a different way—part-time or choosing other options.

In the 1970s, women entered the workforce in slowly increasing numbers, and several things happened to change the way we viewed maternity leave. In 1973 the first EEOC guidelines about pregnancy appeared. This created a considerable stir among American employers. In 1978 the Pregnancy Discrimination Act, which amended Title VIE of the Civil Rights Act, was signed into law. Again, this took pregnancy and women in a different direction.

Leave Concept Broadens

Large numbers of women entered the workforce in the 1980s and people first began to look at leave policy in broader terms. We also began to hear talk about job sharing, part-time work and flextime. It is not surprising that these concepts were being discussed because demographics were rapidly changing.

In the late 1970s and 1980s, many companies started to take a serious look at leave. And in 1985 Congresswoman Patricia Schroeder introduced legislation called the Family and Medical Leave Act. (The federal bill is still pending.) This was the first time many people began thinking about leave for individuals other than pregnant women. With the introduction of this bill, there was a flurry of private sector activity, including the revelation of time off policies. Employers wanted to beat the legislation by developing their own options.

At the same time, there was state government activity. Many states closely followed the course of the federal bill. Several states introduced their own versions of family or parental leave statutes in 1986. And in 1987 Rhode Island was the first state to pass such a statute. Thirteen states have passed legislation since then. The state statutes have created a complex situation for companies with employees in more than one jurisdiction; now they must deal with a varied menu of state rules. On May 14, 1990, the House passed its version of the Family and Medical Leave Act. It provides up to 12 weeks of job-guaranteed unpaid leave for: the birth or adoption of children; care for sick family members; or for the workers own medical illness.

This bill would apply to companies with 50 or more workers at one site and would affect employees who have worked at least 1000 hours in the 12 months prior to taking the leave. Today, June 14, the bill is being debated in the Senate.

Allen W. Bergerson
Director, Personnel Policy Development
Eastman Kodak Company

During the last two years, Kodak has been actively implementing family-friendly programs, two of which address the need for parents to be away from work—both for short and long periods of time. Kodak's senior management established a task force in November 1986 to examine work-family issues and to make policy recommendations. Like other companies, this was a business decision driven by changing demographics, a diverse workforce and increasing competition for quality employees.

Family Leave Program

Our family leave program provides up to 17 weeks of unpaid leave for the birth or adoption of a child. It can also be used for the serious illness of a child, spouse, parents or spouse's parents. In some cases it has been extended to include care of a grandparent or surrogate parent. Health benefits continue during the leave period provided that the employee maintains the co-share portion of premium costs. This is not a discretionary program, but an entitlement. We guarantee a job on the employee's return.

As for utilization, through December 1989, 658 employees of a total population of 83,000 had taken leave. About half are in the age group represented by the childbearing and rearing years. This is not an overwhelming number. But it meets a critical need for the people who took the option. Almost 40 men chose to take leave, about 6 percent of the total. Women took an average leave of 13.8 weeks and men took 12 weeks. Not everyone returns. Over 80 people terminated employment while on family leave, 79 women and three men. So there is some risk. You must be a risk-taker, however, to insure the program's flexibility.

Alternate Work Schedules

We began our alternate work schedule in November 1988. It is the centerpiece of our flexible, away-from-work programs. The program is not an entitlement but we made it as flexible as possible. Supervisors have complete flexibility to accommodate family needs as long as the arrangement does not impact adversely on their business.

The program offers flexibility in four ways:

(1) The employee's current work hours can be adjusted to a more satisfactory permanent schedule.

(2) If it is a short-term care situation, we can be flexible on a day-to-day basis.

(3) Part-time schedules and job sharing are major options in the program.

(4) All the programs are interlinked and a large number of leave configurations are possible.

A typical configuration is that the parent of a newborn uses the paid medical disability leave portion first. It is part of our short-term disability package. This usually runs eight to ten weeks. For approved medical reasons, we can grant up to 26 weeks with full pay and benefits for an employee with fewer than 15 years service and 52 weeks for employees with 15 years or more service. Generally the mother returns to her regular job at the end of the paid short-term disability period.

Susan F. Geisenheimer

Vice President, Human Resources
Time Inc. Magazines

Time Inc. Magazines has a long tradition of being family supportive. Our time off policy is but one of a broad range of work-family programs initiated by the company. As early as 1963, Time offered a six-month unpaid leave for new mothers. At that time, however, women were expected to begin their leave three months before the baby was due.

Parental Leave

In 1971 maternity leave was extended to 12 months; in 1973 leave for adoption was granted; and in 1986 maternity leave changed to parental leave, which meant fathers could use leave. Women giving birth receive between 8-12 weeks paid disability. Women or men can take 12 months of unpaid leave. In unpaid leave, employees receive full medical benefits and return to the same or comparable job. In almost all cases, it is the mother who takes parental leave. Most women return within six months. Fathers tend to use their vacation time, which runs three to four weeks for all employees.

We encourage managers to work with employees who request parental leave. We want them to talk frankly about the length of time employees think they will be on leave, who will do the work while they are gone, whether they will be available for phone calls at home, and how the responsibilities will be transferred. We think it is appropriate to ask these questions because we believe the company has a right to know what the employee wants to do just as the employee has a right to the leave.

I encourage my HR staff to explore alternate work schedules: job sharing; part-time work; four-day work weeks; three days at the office, one day at home; two weeks out of three weeks, and so on. With the arrival of the PC and fax, it has become much easier to work at home. We are therefore experimenting more and more with alternate schedules. For many employees, particularly women, a flexible schedule for the first three or four months after returning from parental leave insures a successful transition.

Putting Ideas Into Practice

Making The Case For A Work-Family Response

[Moderator Ilene R. Gochman, Vice President and General Manager, Organizational Research Practice, Opinion Research Corporation, opened the session by underlining the need to develop work-family programs within the framework of a company's culture.]

Julie Fasone Holder

Group Marketing Manager for Formulation Products Dow Chemical Co.

Dow's effort to address work-family issues has been a six-year process. We are headquartered in Midland, Michigan and our culture reflects a Midwestern, conservative tradition.

Line management drives our organization. Human resources is a support function and has gained impact only in the last five years. We are white male dominated. Women comprise 26 percent of the employees; of the exempt workforce, 18 percent are women and 10 percent minorities. Each division and function has much autonomy. On the one hand, this makes it easier to get things done on a local level, but it makes corporate-wide initiatives difficult to sell and implement. Resistance at the local level can impede progress.

Our work-family policies evolve from Dow's interest in valuing diversity as a way to attract top people. Family issues are one part of the valuing-diversity pie. Other issues we are dealing with include career development for women and minorities and K-12 education. We hope to stimulate interest in math and science particularly so there will be future engineers and chemists for Dow to recruit.

Starting From the Bottom

Dow's work-family efforts trickled up from the bottom, probably the only way it could happen in our culture. Individual efforts were responsible for the beginnings; different people sold the program in small pieces at a time. They were able to persuade the right people that change was needed—but in small increments. Momentum grew as the issue was validated and became a significant business issue. Our progress is slow but steady. Those of us involved have been impatient at times. Looking back, however, we have certainly progressed and a shift has occurred.

We began in 1984. After Workforce 2000 appeared, our top management expressed interest in child care and employee assistance issues. After a presentation on the relevance of work-family issues to the company's future, the Dow board's Public Interest Committee approved the formation of a child care task force. The first step involved employee research. We ran focus groups by function and location to examine employee needs; once the data was gathered, we began looking for solutions. Because we are a major player in our communities, it was critical to have community support. And we got it. We implemented our first effort at corporate headquarters, a pilot resource and referral system called Child Care Concepts.

In 1986 and early 1987, we focused on another issue. Our retention rates for women and minorities were low; we were not succeeding in moving them up the corporate ladder. A number of functions and locations began doing their own employee research as well. As a result, local efforts began to address these concerns. Women formed networking groups in local sales offices and manufacturing sites, as well as at corporate headquarters, to deal with internal communications and mentoring issues. Presentations were made to middle management to heighten their awareness of sexual bias and the lack of value on diversity.

Engaging Top Management

At the same time, top management sanctioned formal activity for the first time by setting up an EEO steering committee. It was made up of line managers from different functions and manufacturing divisions. The group made recommendations in five key areas: training—starting with managers and eventually all employees; internal communication; organizational resources, including our structure for managing diversity; incorporating mentoring and accountability for people managers; and establishing goals and measures. One of our key recommendations was that diversity training begin at the top. The U.S. area operating board and other members of our executive committee were the first to participate in a one-day training program.

In January 1990, our executive management articulated a new company vision: Dow U.S.A. is a team of exceptional, diverse, and highly motivated people who continuously improve and innovate for customer success. Because our vision addresses the need for a diverse workforce, we can now tie our activities to the corporate vision. Work-family issues have become a legitimate business issue.

We have learned these lessons:
• Take small steps; be patient about significant change.
• Sell diversity as you would any business issue— by doing employee research and highlighting such issues as turnover, retention, recruiting and training, and the loss of return on investment.
• Limit emotional pleas; be rational and logical; persistence and consistency is key.
• Get top management support so you can work the top and bottom against the middle; expect to stumble at middle management levels.
• Expect backlash; men are concerned because they fear minorities and women will get promoted over them; some women feel the increased attention is not to their benefit.

If you don't act until everyone is on board, you will probably never act. For Dow, the best way to address work-family issues is to take incremental steps, stay the course, and let the momentum build.

Ellen Galinsky
Co-Founder and Co-President
Families and Work Institute

Our research shows that companies go through different stages of evolution in the development of work-family programs. In stage one, someone raises the issue of work-family within the company. It isn't a popular issue; the immediate response is resistance. At first it is assumed to be a child care issue, a women's issue, which creates equity problems. The company assumes you are talking about an on-site care center, and management doesn't want to face the cost and liability factors. This is the beginning of stage one. A champion then arises in the company; either top-down or bottom-up champions may surface. The champion begins to make a business case.

Productivity and Work-Family Issues

The first question asked is, How do child care problems affect productivity? Our research findings address a number of different factors. The first is finding out about available care in the community. In our study for Fortune magazine, we found that one in every five parents had a difficult time getting adequate child care information; with infants, it was one in four parents. In all our research, having difficulty either locating quality care or getting into the program is the most significant predictor of absenteeism. There is a link between problems with finding child care and being at work.

The second significant predictor of productivity relates to the fact that some child care arrangements are more satisfactory than others. The National Child Care Staffing study found that the average care children receive in this country is barely adequate. We looked at whether the quality of care affects parents on the job. We found a non-significant link for infants. But for parents of preschoolers, there was a significant relationship between parents of children in poor quality programs and the amount of stress they had. Our measure for stress also assesses stress-related health problems.

We also know that the type of care affects productivity, particularly with latchkey children. We found a group of qualities—center location, how flexible it is, whether the parents had input into decision making—to be predictive of parents' stress and stress-related problems.

The next issue is that parents make multiple selections for child care. They put together patchwork arrangements. The more arrangements parents have, the more likely they are to fall apart. In our study for Fortune, 40 percent of the parents had at least one breakdown in child care arrangements within the last three months, and one out of four parents had two to five breakdowns within the last three months. We have found that having to cope with more frequent child care breakdowns is correlated with missing work altogether, arriving late, leaving early, spending unproductive time at work, more stress and stress-related health problems, more tension and less companionship in marriage and feeling less effective as parents.

The second question in stage one is, Isn't this a women's issue? Women do have higher levels of absenteeism; but when the kids get older, men's levels of absenteeism rise. Men also are participating more in the care of sick children. In a needs assessment, we found that 27 percent of the men and 49 percent of the women missed work at least once. Women have more stress related to child care; this is because they take the greatest responsibility. We are beginning to see a shift here. Research shows that when men take an equal amount of responsibility for caring, they aren't immune to stress.

Evolution of Work-Family Programs

In stage one—based on our findings—companies typically establish resource and referral services, flexible spending accounts or parent seminars. Does the solution affect productivity? There are now 17 empirical studies about the productivity effects—particularly related to on-site child care—and they find that the major benefit is the ability to recruit and retain employees.

In stage two, companies move away from the exclusive issue of child care and become interested in elder care as well. They begin to frame these issues as dependent care. Elder care responsibilities increase stress, decrease leisure time, increase conflict between work and family responsibilities, and this all impacts productivity. Elder caregivers often cut back on their hours. The New York Business Group on Health found that almost 40 percent cut back; 33 percent came in late or left early.

Companies also tackle the issue of time in stage two. Most people don't work a 40-hour week. According to our Fortune survey, 61 percent of men and 27 percent of women work more than 45 hours a week. The number of hours is a particular problem for men, the scheduling of hours is more problematical for women. Studies have shown that flexibility ensures more time for the family, but this depends largely on the degree of flexibility. Flexibility can reduce stress, reduces absenteeism and tardiness, and improve morale.

Another issue at stage two is training the supervisors and educating middle management. Our research shows four descriptors of a supportive supervisor:

(1) Knowing the work-family policies.

(2) Applying the policies without favoritism.

(3) Showing flexibility when work-family problems arise.

(4) Believing work-family is a legitimate part of the workplace.

The boss's attitude about whether or not women should work is one of the most important predictors of how men and women handle work-family problems and how employees are treated. One study found that having a supportive supervisor when you have just had a baby is as important as having a supportive husband in terms of managing the transition.

In a nutshell, companies are taking a more holistic approach, tackling the tougher issues in stage two. The motivation here relates to recruitment and retention.

In stage three, companies begin to see work-family as a continuous process. And they begin to integrate work-family with other areas of the company. They include career development or affirmative action, for example. They also begin to improve the quality of child care within their community.

Examples of stage three companies include AT&T, Johnson & Johnson, and IBM. AT&T's $10 million negotiated fund allows employees to work with community organizations to jointly apply for funds. They fund efforts to increase the supply and improve the quality of local child care. Johnson & Johnson has just announced a pilot study that tries to serve under-served children. IBM has a $22 million fund dedicated to expanding and improving child care. The motivation for these efforts is the future workforce. Companies realize that the baby bust generation is here and that they must do something to improve the quality of its early experiences in order to be competitive in the 21st century.

We have much to learn. Many questions about the complex issue of work and family remain unanswered.

Fitting Programs to Workforce Needs

[Moderator Jean A. Fraser, Vice President, Employee Relations, American Express Company, introduced the session with brief comments about the most difficult concept to implement—flexibility—because it requires a culture shift.]

Martha Montag Brown
Director, Community Affairs
Levi Strauss & Co.

Levi Strauss is the world's largest apparel manufacturer. Women are the majority of its workforce. Our company mission is to sustain profitable and responsible commercial success with responsible being the key word in terms of work-family.

Our work-family program now includes: a child care information and referral program; the development of an on-site child care center in a Canadian facility; child care leave for men or women for birth or adoption; sick leave for dependent care; flextime, job sharing and part-time. And the Levi Strauss Foundation supports a funding program for child and elder care in Levi's plant communities worldwide.

We are now making a renewed effort because of changing demographics, labor shortages and competitiveness. We call it "baby boom II" partly because we have increasing numbers of women in key management positions who are taking maternity leave. This has heightened the issue among management because we don't want to lose these women.

Changing production cycles have also brought pressures on management. In our industry we don't have factories where people necessarily come to work at eight and leave at five. There are times during the year when people work 12 hours a day and times when they don't work at all. This wreaks havoc with personal life. Employees have been telling management that this is increasingly difficult in the face of child and elder care needs. In many of our communities, there are no child or elder care services for people on the night shift or for those who come to work at 6 a.m.

A Company-Wide Program

To fit the program to our workforce needs, we realized that we had to do a wholesale review, a company-wide program. We wanted to be sure that we didn't produce another home office program and roll it out to the field. We wanted to ensure that we had the participation, support and ownership of people company-wide. Our renewed effort is a collaboration between the human resources department, the community affairs and foundation departments, the employee assistance and benefits departments, operations and marketing.

We agreed on a task force approach. We decided that the best way for us to proceed would be to form a group representative of the workforce and charge this group to lead, construct, review, critique and roll out the work-family program.

Senior management support and participation are critical for change. We knew we needed their involvement. And we have it. Bob Haas, the chairman of the board and CEO, participates on our work-family task force and has made the program one of his key 1990 objectives. As co-chair of the work-family task force, I meet quarterly with each of the members of our executive management committee to keep them involved and informed and to provide them an opportunity for input.

A Diverse Task Force

We were strongly committed to an effective task force. We carefully selected a group of people to work with us, an ethnically and racially diverse group that also represents family diversity—single parents, work-ing mothers and fathers, a gay person, a single person, a pregnant person and people with elder care concerns. In addition, we selected people with different job functions—a sewing machine operator, the chairman of the board, a sales rep, a line manager, a middle manager in the home office, a secretary etc. We wanted people who would speak up to represent their colleagues and enrich the process.

To make a difference, our corporate culture must change to support this program. Employees should not feel that they must work seven days a week to be successful or that to go home to care for a dependent is inappropriate. Changing corporate culture challenges assumptions like those of some production managers who might tell us that there is no place in a factory for flexibility. They are beginning to see that this is not true.

Our task force mission is to create an environment company-wide where employees can better balance their work and personal lives. Our specific objectives are to assess the needs of our employees, to articulate a vision for the company based on these needs, and to review and recommend appropriate program and policy strategies.

A Customized Survey

Information gathering is a key part of fitting the program to workforce needs. We are conducting a broad survey that is being field tested now. We have questions on child and elder care, management attitudes, company culture. From this, we will collect data from each site and determine what specific workforce needs exist. We are pulling people off the floor to conduct the survey. To get data as specific as possible, we are doing a separate, customized survey for our sales force, our home office staff, our hourly employees, and for managers and non-managers. We have invested heavily in focus groups. We have run 18 focus groups just to help us design the survey. We will conduct focus groups once the survey is completed to help clarify what employees have said.

For this program to succeed and ensure that it fits workplace needs, strong commitment and involvement from our senior management is critical. At the same time, the task force is an effective check-and-balance mechanism that helps us stay on track. The task force provides us increased credibility in the company as a whole because it isn't simply corporate staff dreaming up new plans. Rather it comes from all the employees.

We want to be sure we aren't misleading people or raising expectations unfairly. We won't have a child care center at every site or subsidize each employee's child or elder care program. We must communicate the kinds of programs we expect to develop. As a task force, we want our recommendations to be approved. If we recommend fancy, expensive programs, they won't be approved; a key company focus is on cost-containment. The issue becomes existing resources of both time and money. We are asking that they be directed differently, in a way that gives each employee more control.

Michael A. Snipes
Compensation and Benefits Director
Allstate Insurance Company

Allstate, a company that is 49 percent women, introduced a national resource and referral service in 1986 called Child Care Solutions. We shaped this program based mainly on employee feedback sessions. It is designed to assist employees with child care needs. Solutions features a toll-free child care hotline staffed by trained counselors who answer questions or assist with problems. Counselors provide information on licensed and registered child caregivers in local communities. Solutions also disseminates resource material on choosing, managing and paying for child care. Parenting workshops are conducted at Allstate locations and present ideas for easing the role of working parents. Through this national referral service, Allstate has provided financial assistance in developing and educating child care providers in nationwide sites.

Conducting a Planning Survey

We conducted a major research and planning survey of 2,300 employees in 1988 to determine their child care needs. It was a telephone survey with interviews usually running 30 minutes each. Among the selected findings were: 39 percent of the employees report that a spouse or other household member cares for the children; 26 percent use an outside source; only 20 percent use day care centers; employees expressed concern about latchkey children; 49 percent arrived late or left early due to child care problems; 63 percent said that a family member would stay home in the event of a sick child, using either a floating holiday or a vacation day. Employees indicated they want more workplace flexibility as far as sick child care. These are all productivity issues.

Allstate also conducted child care focus groups throughout the U.S. in 1988. We solicited feedback from employees as well as management staff. With this information, we conceptualized our first work and family model. We introduced the program during our first quarter. We wanted to be sure management—who would supervise the program—understood, communicated and raised questions about how the program should work.

This model, Work and Family Connections, has five components:
(1) Employment policies
(2) Information and referral services
(3) A flexible spending account program
(4) Wellness and safety programs
(5) Educational services
In phase one, we introduced an integrated family leave, EAP, school match programs, child referral services, and emphasized flexible work schedules and job sharing. As we implemented phase one in 1989, we almost immediately began developing phase two. We felt it was important, for example, to do a survey of child care referral users. We received favorable responses from these users. We ran more focus groups in selected locations and developed our phase two model.

Planning a Work and Family Strategy

We are dealing with work and family strategy in phase two. This is a multi-step process in which planning is key. It is important to have an ongoing dialogue and get the support of key constituencies. Data analysis is also critical because, as our initial survey revealed, there are often mixed messages.

In trying to frame all this, a mission statement was developed. Our future goal is to build a competitive advantage by creating an environment that recognizes and supports work and family issues. This links to Allstate's other social commitments; we have sponsored national forums, for example, on AIDS, public education and related issues. We want to be a premier employer; we want to attract and retain the best employees and maximize productivity.

Top management is very supportive of these programs. Some middle managers, however, are having difficulty trying to manage some of it and still face productivity issues. We must help managers understand the importance of work and family needs and learn how to deal with them sensitively and flexibly. A major finding in our surveys was that management flexibility is a key issue. We will continue to emphasize flexibility in the workplace.

We also want to revisit our family illness policy. Many employees who take a family illness day feel penalized for doing so. This is a cultural issue and we must work with our managers. In the child care area, we are doing a needs analysis. Directly related to this, five Allstate sites have been selected to participate in a study. We will explore the feasibility of establishing near or on-site child care centers in these locations. The assessment process will include employee focus groups, site analysis, and surveys and interviews with management at each location. We are forming a strategic task force. We must have all departments involved, especially our claims and sales departments, to help define and refine work and family strategies.

Work and family is a continuing process. It requires the effort and involvement of many employee groups and top management to ensure that it works and meets specific business needs.

After Implementation: Evaluating and Fine Tuning

Arlene A. Johnson
Senior Research Associate
The Conference Board, Inc.

In the field of work and family policies, we see marked changes in recent years. Not too long ago we spent most of the time "making the case." We, of course, remain involved in defining the business rationale, but increasingly time and effort is spent evaluating the programs in place and exploring how they play in different cultures. What happens when work and family issues are no longer just a cause to fight for but a process to manage? Where is creativity and innovation possible in the implementation process?

Some of the developing issues are:
• Comunicating; helping managers and employees understand what you are up to.
• Determining the role of consultants versus the role of company staff; how much you want to internalize or externalize this process.
• Deciding what is legitimate criteria for evaluating success; how to assess and monitor programs.
• Identifying the need for program modification.
• Managing expectations and frustrations; if the program is oversold or if the implementation is slow or if the culture is reluctant to catch up with the program.

We know some things don't work. Even the best policy cannot substitute for getting the details right. After you have done a needs assessment and developed a plan, it is a mistake to stick rigidly to the original plan. And we know that it doesn't work to begin implementation without adequate training and support, because these are complex problems and culture change issues.

Deborah Stahl
Director, Family Care Development Fund
AT&T

In January 1990, AT&T began to implement—for the first time—a company-wide, comprehensive package of family-supportive benefits. Since those initiatives are so new, we are actively involved in the process of evaluation and fine tuning. AT&T's work-family story, however, begins in the late 60s. Along with other industries, we started to study the causes of employee losses, costs of high turnover and the difficulties involved in hiring qualified people. There was little hard data available on the corporate benefits of work and family programs.

Experiment in the 1970s

Two experimental on-site child care centers were created in 1971: one in Washington, D.C. and the other in Columbus, Ohio. Both centers failed by every measure you can imagine. Employee interest was minimal; enrollment was low; and research didn't reveal any cost savings in terms of retention or productivity to offset the cost of the operation. The Washington center closed after three years and the Columbus center in less than two years.

The reasons for this failure seem to be that the centers addressed the needs of only a small percentage of the company's parents. Both centers were in urban settings and many parents who commuted from the suburbs didn't want to bring their children into the city. In short, these centers were a singular response to a complex problem. Because of this inauspicious start, there was a long period at AT&T when the topic of child care triggered the response, "We tried that once and it just didn't work."

Response in the 1980s

AT&T didn't begin to respond formally to work-family issues again until the mid-1980s. One of the main reasons was the divestiture of the Bell System in 1984. AT&T spun off its 22 local telephone companies and the largest corporate reorganization in American history was underway. Inevitably work-family issues took a back seat to such concerns as job security and market-place survival. But as the corporate world absorbed the implications of Workforce 2000, pressures to act on family care issues quickly began to build.

A corporate task force formed in 1986 as employee groups expressed their concerns to top management. Since about two-thirds of AT&T employees are represented by the CWA and IBEW unions, it became clear that a wide-ranging set of initiatives would have to be created at the bargaining table. The goal was to develop a viable package for the 1989 contract negotiations.

In its facilities across the U.S., AT&T launched a number of trial programs —support of local child care centers, development of resource and referral services, etc.—and they enjoyed great success. A comprehensive needs assessment was also conducted. Both the pilots and the needs assessment underscored the need for a comprehensive range of benefits. Based on this evaluation and in partnership with their unions in a remarkably smooth round of negotiations in May 1989, AT&T shaped its package of family-supportive benefits.

Among the program's features are:

• A nationwide child care resource and referral program
• An elder care program of consultation and referral
• Unpaid leave, up to a full year with benefits paid for six months and a job guarantee upon return, for care of a newborn or a seriously-ill family member
• An expanded employee assistance program that includes immediate family members
• Family Care Development Fund, a three-year $10 million grantmaking project aimed at increasing the supply of improving the quality of community child and elder care for AT&T employees

The process of evaluation and fine tuning is ongoing. Today we have a good set of programs and strong top-level commitment. AT&T's managers are increasingly aware of the business reasons for investing in work-family programs. Today we find ourselves in far fewer discussions about why we are doing this and more discussions about how we can do it better.

Gerald F. Murray

Chief, Air Force Family Policy
Research, Training and Long-Range Plans
United States Air Force

Anxious to identify key factors in their retention slide since the late 1970s, the U.S. Air Force contracted numerous studies to determine why people were leaving the Air Force. Research documented three related findings:

(1) The Air Force had changed from a predominantly single force to one in which more than two-thirds had family responsibilities.
(2) The families were not traditional nuclear families.
(3) Family-member attitudes toward military life, especially the spouse's, were a major factor in the employee's decision to remain or leave.

Family Support Centers

Responding to these findings, the Air Force launched its initial efforts in the work-family area. Recommendations from conferences held in the early 1980s led to the development of Family Support Centers (FSC) worldwide. The FSCs are the cornerstone of the Air Force family support system and provide a broad range of services, including inform –

ation and referral services; relocation, spouse employment and crisis assistance; and services to families with special needs. FSCs have been a major success story for the Air Force. They recorded over a million contacts last year. And research shows they are positively impacting retention and productivity.

After the initial implementation, however, there were indications that the scope of our success was limited. Surveys showed that issues such as spouse employment and relocation continued to be problems for families. At the same time, FSC administration at the division and local levels tended to focus exclusively on the employee rather than family members. Line and other HR organizations were not addressing work-family issues. Rather, they were simply sending people to the FSC to get "fixed." Our effectiveness was in jeopardy because the corporation mainstream had not substantially changed its attitude toward families.

As a direct result of these pressures on the FSCs, the Chief of Staff—the Air Force's CEO—chartered a panel to evaluate the Air Force's family support system. The panel conducted an exhaustive review and, among other recommendations, developed the following program criteria:

(1) The program should ensure a focus on families.
(2) The program should be proactive and prevention-oriented.
(3) The program should aim at assisting management in creating a more family-friendly work environment.

The Air Force was moving its family support system into what Galinsky and Friedman call the second and third stages of work-family program development. The second stage is characterized by integration of services in the organization. By institutionalizing policy, planning and coordination, we would enable all parts of the system to work together to provide integrated programs and services. The third stage is characterized by changing the culture. Our cultural focus now is as much on how the organization can change to accommodate family well-being as it is on what families can do to adjust to work environment stresses.

Although the program specifics didn't change much, how the programs are approached has changed significantly. Our new program views the family as the service unit. It also recognizes the need to provide comprehensive services to meet the needs of diverse family models in different stages of the life cycle. At first, there was considerable resistance to this evolution in the Air Force family program.

Work-family program development is an evolutionary process. Management will be quick, at a number of checkpoints along the way, to consider the job finished. It is essential to the long-term success of work-family initiatives to build an evaluation component into every step of the process. We must clearly define what we intend to accomplish and continually evaluate whether we are succeeding or not. If not, why not? We must always ask ourselves, How can we do this better?

When You're Ready to Change the Culture

Karen A. Geiger
Director, Career Development
NCNB Corporation

No matter what policies you have in place, the corporate culture will either make or break the success of these policies. Think about your own corporate culture because it is unique for each company. The first thing to do when considering work-family issues is to define where your company is, identify what policies are already in place, and compare how these mesh with what your corporation says it needs.

Then implement some new policies. Once these policies are in place, the culture is critical; it has much to do with the successful integration of the new policies. If the culture doesn't support these policies, they will have no credibility for your employees. A non-supportive culture can undermine all your best intentions and efforts.

Your company culture already has values about balancing work and family, whether or not they are stated. Values are operative that are clear to the company's employees. Culture can be visible and tangible. You may have a written ethical code, a mission statement, a stated corporate vision, a credo. This is the official culture, the values of the corporation's founder or today's top management. These ideas may not be valued, however, by the informal network. The unofficial culture may contradict the mission statement. Frequently, there is a differentiation between the official and operating culture.

Rethinking the Values

Social changes and shifting demographic patterns require examination of the traditional values found in most corporate cultures. Among these old values are:
- Managers focus on time spent at the office rather than on results.
- Extended time off is seen as lack of dedication to the job rather than as assuming family responsibility.
- Career development means moving up the hierarchy rather than assuming more challenging and varied work.
- Personal and family issues are left at home.
- At the policy level, people are treated in the aggregate rather than with flexibility.

- Companies focus on short-term productivity rather than long-term employee retention.
- If a man is a real man, he puts aside family values and is at work rather than caring for his parents or children.

How do you change old values to new? Cultures are always evolving. No single set of solutions will apply. You may implement imaginative policies, but there will always be managers who won't buy them and must be persuaded.

Rewriting the Culture

You can change the culture explicitly. You can rewrite credos, mission statements, ethical codes, policies, or circulate statements and speeches by top management that express the new values. Company newsletters, press releases, annual reports and corporate histories are all vehicles to put it in writing. Send it to everyone—internally and externally. These kinds of materials get read and heard, particularly in companies where people "want to go by the book." Give them a new book—a flexible one.

You can audit your culture to determine exactly what it is. This is very complicated but worth the effort. You can also mount a massive resocialization. This involves hiring, formal training, appraisal and reward systems, using certain employees as role models and reinforcing your stated values with field experiences. If you hire good people, for example, into less than full-time schedules and point out how well they are doing, this in itself supports a culture statement that says you value results and not time spent at work. In existing management training, you can insert information and applications of the new work-family policies to create structure around all the flexibility.

Rewarding the Flexible

Look at performance appraisals of people who leave at five p.m. to pick up children or take leaves of absence. Determine if they are being appraised negatively for these practices. The reward systems need to be watched carefully. Bonuses, incentives and salary increases can be managed and monitored. They should be awarded to employees who manage flexibly. This is one of the best ways to affirm a particular value. People can't be knocked out of the incentive system because they work a flexible schedule. The schedule needs to be pro-rated, and we need to evaluate their results in light of the incentive plans.

Expect resistance when you change the culture. You are asking people to change their values, and values arouse strong feelings. Beliefs about gender roles, for example, are very powerful. It isn't enough to simply state that men can take paternity leave. We are talking mainly about middle management resistance here. Support from the top is potent, but people in the middle can subtly sabotage what top management is saying and doing. Don't forget these people if you really want your policies to work.

Thomas E. Blumer

Director, Human Resource Planning and
Development
Corning Inc.

At Corning we do not talk about work and family issues. We talk about valuing diversity. When we talk about a subset of valuing diversity, we talk about career and family. There is a subtle distinction between work and career. When I think about work, I think about tasks; career makes me think of a long-term commitment and investment. So when we talk about work and family, we in fact talk about our career and family balancing programs. And we put it in the context of valuing diversity.

Corning began developing its valuing-diversity focus in 1986 for five reasons:

(1) Our values statement, which is founded on the value of the individual; we want each employee to grow to his or her fullest personal and professional potential.

(2) Our quality process; we introduced the total quality concept to the corporation in 1983.

(3) The changing demographics; the shrinking workforce makes our recruiting efforts tougher each year.

(4) Our loss of women at twice the rate of white males; this represented an attrition loss costing $3.5-4 million a year.

(5) Our inability to translate recruiting success into career development success; people were leaving because they felt there were no opportunities and they were stagnating.

Conflict of Old Values and New Initiatives

A strong work ethic has always been one of Corning's values. It encourages team work, organizational pride and accomplishment. As we started digging into this particular cultural value, we found that some elements conflicted with what we were trying to do with diversity and career-family balancing. Before 1986, for example, we measured how much time was spent on the job, not on what was produced. As far as appropriate behavior and attitude, it was taboo to leave work and pick up children from school or the caregiver. Parents leaving at 5 p.m. to pick up a child were perceived as being more loyal to the family than to the

company. So certain areas of our corporate culture were getting in our way.

Some other important values at Corning in 1986 were: paying your dues (taking the lousy job in an undesirable location); being a polite, conservative organization. Historically it has been a male company; before 1986 no women worked in management. And family issues were equated with women's issues. Much of our corporate behavior and social norms contradicted our diversity effort and our career and family balancing initiatives.

Although the 1986 culture didn't support our diversity and career-family efforts, James Houghton, our CEO, was and is strongly committed to the change. He has provided the necessary kinds of communications, financial support and management backing to ensure that cultural change happened. The key word is support.

The solution was to change the culture. And we started to do this in 1986. At the corporate level, we formed a quality improvement team. They met to verify what the culture issues were and to develop initiatives that would make Corning a family-friendly place. At the local level, we created corrective action teams that focused on the same issues. Training was a key element of our cultural change mechanism. In addition to the support programs we implemented, we made changes in our compensation system, our appraisal system and our communications strategy. In each corporate communication there is at least one reference to our career-family and diversity programs.

Men and Women as Colleagues

Our valuing diversity training was the major element of our culture change. We developed a course titled Men and Women as Colleagues. It was taught top-down. We started with the CEO and his staff. As a result of this course, we had a story to tell. The CEO, his committee and other key members of senior management gave up their weekend to talk about these issues. Corning's managers don't teach the course; we feel it must be facilitated externally.

The course is divided into four sections. The first looks at gender issues from a global perspective. Then we talk about the myths; for example, only men get hired and promoted at Corning, only women take care of children. We then discuss socialization, look at how we all grew up. We look at our own biases and at the dynamics of why we act as we do. We then look at organizational norms—what are those things in the culture that impact us? We discuss how to recognize issues and how to change behaviors.

A single course isn't going to change the culture. But the right course will start the cultural change. Most managers entered the course thinking there was no problem because they had never seen it. They leave the course realizing that they are part of the problem. The impact is powerful. Both men and women cry as they discover their own behaviors. It confirms the gender issues that we all believe have been there. The most important point that emerges is that career and family needs more work. We must continue knocking down barriers to balancing career and family.

We have seen behavior start to change. Organizations are starting to identify their own issues. Each unit in every company has a subculture of the major organizational culture. As you start impacting at the unit level, you really begin to change the organization and the culture.

Since implementation in 1986, we have seen attrition cut in half. This is about a $2 million annual savings. Most important is that we have put the issues on the table. It is now okay to talk about career and family. We are also experiencing flexibility. We use every form of alternative work schedules at Corning today; two years ago we didn't. Another critical result is that there has been a subtle perception change. The issue of career and family is no longer seen as a women's issue. Women championed it, but now men are supporting it so that they can help carry it along.

Michael J. Carey
Vice President, Human Resources
Johnson & Johnson Personal Products Company

In Megatrends, John Naisbitt said that change occurs when there is a confluence of both changing values and economic necessity, not before. The work and family movement is in the process of proving his point again. The fact is that our sympathy as a people is not enough to bring about social change in an economic context. Companies aren't founded or managed for social altruism. We are money-making enterprises.

We started looking at work-family issues in the late 1980s. We understood that family conflicts affect productivity; and we knew we had to build employee feelings of ownership and commitment. We established a task force in October 1987 to examine work-family issues. Our mission was to achieve a better understanding of the changing relationship between corporations and families and to identify Johnson & Johnson's business objectives in addressing these issues. We were to define the framework within which to recommend initiatives.

We wanted to include our employees in this process so we conducted extensive research for one full year. Surveys focused on the need for a child care center but covered a broad range of work and family issues. We conducted a number of focus groups involving several hundred employees. The research findings told us that

employees wanted more flexibility in the workplace, consistency in the application of policies, and help in fulfilling child and elder care responsibilities. We learned that our environment, supervisors, programs and policies weren't as family-sensitive as we wanted them to be.

The task force identified elements needed to change the environment and culture:
- We must get top management support; they must believe in the change.
- We must respond to changing needs.
- We must establish a program that offers care for all generations—children, spouses, elders.
- We must provide benefits for individual needs through a flexible plan.

We considered these issues in the framework of our employees' needs and our ability to pay versus employees' ability to pay. Legal issues and our competitive position were also considered.

The task force submitted its program to Johnson & Johnson's executive committee and it was approved. Among other items, it includes manager and supervisor training; employee assistance support; lifestyle seminars; flexible benefits; a nationwide resource and referral system for child care and elder care; adoption assistance program; one-year family care leave with benefits; paid family care absences for emergencies; and finally, alternative work arrangements. Policy changes had to be implemented, but first we had to train managers in the new policies. The programs were announced and put in place. In March 1989, after the recommendations were approved, we announced the change in Johnson and Johnson's Credo—our values statement. More than anything else, this was a signal to management and employees that we meant business.

Our former chairman said that we wanted people to know that this program was "real and forever." We taped him discussing these issues and interviewed the incoming chairman as well—so there would be no doubts about continuity. These tapes were used in the dissemination of the management philosophy in a mailing to the homes of all 32,000 U.S.-based employees. The letter from chairman Jim Burke said in part:

> It is becoming a growing challenge in our society to manage a career while raising a family and perhaps caring for aging parents at the same time...We must support these efforts. To provide support, we are initiating a comprehensive effort of new policies, programs and services to help meet the challenges of balancing work and family...The Credo incorporates new language in which our commitment to helping employees meet their family responsibility is clearly stated.

The new Credo says, "We must be mindful of ways to help our employees fulfill their family responsibilities." The agenda to support this change encourages a partnership between employee and supervisor. This was not to be a paternalistic approach. Rather, it was a practical partnering toward business solutions necessary for our future.

Working with the Families and Work Institute, we developed a model called Balancing Work and Family. It prescribes an organization that provides a supportive environment, managers with awareness, sensitivity and flexibility, and employees as an integral part of the equation—understanding their role and responsibility. When we outlined our program, we detailed the employee's responsibility. We held discussion groups to talk about the need for people to accept a role in the balancing process.

Before implementation in July 1989, our managers used too many crutches—black and white answers from the policy manual. Many of them deviated from the manual but most systems were rather formalized. We will see a change in culture over time, not overnight. We have the commitment, the leadership and the support systems in place. The work and family task force remains in tact.

We also developed an employee relations managers' council. With a network of 25 companies all managing these issues, we decided to create a formal structure to implement and support them. Now we are examining flexibility issues and pay systems. A child care center opens in May at our New Brunswick site. It is a 200-slot center; and we have just approved a 200-slot center in Somerset County, New Jersey. We will continue moving ahead—through committee work, solving practical problems, and exploring the culture we want for Johnson & Johnson.

Redefining Expectations, Responsibilities and Commitments

Fran S. Rodgers
President
Work/Family Directions

We will look at the big picture, look at work-family issues in the context of an evolving major redefinition of how Americans will work. America's work revolution is occurring for a number of reasons. The rapidly changing business climate and our shifting demographics are two major facts. We want to step back and look at the big picture because it is critical to have a sense of where we are going in order to use the right building blocks to get there.

Looking at the Big Picture

Responding to massive workforce changes means taking dozens of different actions each year. Each of these actions—deciding what to do about child care, parental leave policy, elder care—is a building block toward something bigger. But if we don't know what that something bigger is, how can we make the right choices along the way? The other reason for looking at the big picture is that America is at a crossroads with regard to families. We aren't going to utilize our inherent talents and resources unless we begin to understand how all these issues fit into the jugular business concerns of this country.

The nature of the big picture is that it is hard to define. It raises ambiguities and more questions than it answers. I will focus on women's labor force participation, not because work-family issues are only women's issues but because it is women leaving the home over the last 20 years that has galvanized the work-family movement. Women used to be the support system that allowed men to be productive. As women continue to

leave the home and make choices about what kinds of work they want, this will determine some of the most strategic decisions business will make in the future.

About 20 years ago, a new generation of women entered the labor force. Low-income and poor women always worked, generally in conditions and with pay inferior to men's. But the new generation of women entered the workforce with rather different expectations than previous generations. They entered careers and institutions previously dominated by men. Eventually they expected to reach parity with men at the workplace.

Women in the Workplace, the 1960s-1980s

In the late 1960s and through the 1970s, we grappled with the issue of creating a level playing field for women in entry-level jobs in U.S. corporations. We did a good job. Men opened up jobs to women, and they tried to make the workplace fair. During this period, women were saying that they were more than mothers, that they had ambition and talent, that they wanted to contribute more than their motherhood.

We all advised each other not to talk about family at the workplace, and men complied. And here lies the root of a well-intentioned conspiracy of silence that crept into the work environment about family issues. Not only did we not talk about the family but also we advised each other on how to be just like men—how to dress like them, talk sports like them and so on. Thus, the first decade dealt with teaching women how to behave more like men. Men and women did this together.

In the 1980s, we discovered that community resources weren't adequate and that we had problems with our children. We rediscovered the family. In the early 1980s, we discovered the desperate child care needs that weren't being filled. Toward the end of the decade, we started to notice that elder care needs weren't being filled either—largely because women were no longer in the home. We therefore emphasized programs about dependent care during the 1980s. We looked at child care as an issue and made progress promoting the idea that dependent care issues were workplace issues. We talked about child care, struggled with parental leave policies, and looked at policies that might make it possible for men and women to have parity.

It has become clear that providing programs for dependent care alone isn't enough to really address the fulfillment of female ambition and talent. Sweden, for example, has strong family support but still doesn't see many women in high corporate positions. We have been tinkering, grafting on programs to an unchanging corporate culture and an unchanging core. Despite the revolution in the workforce, career structures are basically the same as when this era began. Criteria for success in companies has changed very little, and the basic culture and work practices have changed little. They were all designed for men with wives at home. The design fit the population of the time.

Stalled in Chaos, the 1990s

In the 1990s, it will be more difficult for women and men who want to do things differently. We are stalled. There isn't an upward curve as we had anticipated. At the beginning of the 1980s, women made great strides in middle management, but as we hit 1990, middle management itself is being obliterated. The numbers aren't getting any better for women breaking through middle management; there has been insignificant change in the number of women moving from the middle into top management.

What will it take to get unstalled? As a society, we understand that everyone must be as productive as possible and we must take advantage of available talent. Since we have serious labor force shortages and an educational gap, we need to employ women and men more fully who must and should also nurture families. One fundamental issue is our career development system, which is dysfunctional for everyone. The hierarchical structures are becoming increasingly difficult to move through for everyone. For women and men who want to care for dependents, it is totally dysfunctional. We cannot continue to behave as though we can train people, wait until a slot is available for them to progress, and then move them up the ladder or across the country. On this point alone, we lose enormous numbers of valuable employees.

We must tie the work-family issue to other business issues. American business is in a bit of chaos about how it should work anyway, so why not throw the work-family issue into the chaos? As companies reduce middle management and give more responsibilities to teams of people, for example, why not give them more control for team scheduling? Companies are willing to delegate responsibility for redesigning products to their employees but they still won't allow them to control tasks that would make their lives more reasonable. This is a missed opportunity.

The greatest challenge is competitiveness. But the first response to competitiveness always is to work people harder and longer. The American family can't take this anymore. People with family responsibility say their families have taken all the hits they can. We have already marginalized family life so much that there is nothing else to give—if we care about our future. We must figure out ways to work people better, not longer.

Derek F. Harvey
Manager, Planning and Administration
Mobil Corporation

Mobil began the 1980s with over 200,000 people and ended the decade with 70,000. We sold non-oil businesses and concentrated and upgraded our mainstream oil divisions. There has been tremendous turbulence. How do we make sense of an issue like work-family within this framework? We have come to work-family issues by examining how they fit in with other strategic human resource issues. We have not had a work-family committee or department.

We started a serious reappraisal of Mobil's human resources policies and programs in 1986. There were two issues at the time. The price of crude had dropped from $28 to $10, which led to a fundamental reassessment of how to make money. And we questioned whether our core human resource programs and policies were relevant for the 90s.

One of the major human resource concerns was career development for women and minorities. We had started our upward mobility programs in the early 70s. Were they relevant? We ran a series of focus groups among Mobil employees; in the groups, women were strongly against making this a women's issue. As we probed, we began to see that what started as an exploration of hindrances became a more fundamental study— of career development, productivity and utilization in general.

Examining Career Development

To expand from the feedback which came from the focus groups we designed a survey instrument that deliberately linked relocation, gender and family issues to Mobil's core career development process. This was more than a work-family survey. Career development was one of Mobil's key strengths; we wanted to look at policies in relation to this strength, not at any single component. We also wrestled with asking family questions. This had never been part of our culture. We were encouraged that IBM had conducted a survey containing family questions. We debated the issue and it was finally decided that we could ask family questions.

We weren't doing this survey in isolation. We were also carrying out studies trying to link management style with workplace productivity and climate. In addition, we were reassessing the validity of our compensation and benefit programs, particularly the issue of pay for performance. We were looking at office locations. Why have offices in so many cities; what does this do to career development, particularly for women? Could we centralize offices? Would there be good financial reasons to do this as well as helping career development?

We thought we had a good career development system. But our employees thought differently. When it came to coaching, communication and individual development, employees said the company was not doing well. This was universal—both sexes, high-potential employees, average people, senior level staff. In the feedback, we also learned attitudes about relocation and related issues. We also discovered concerns about child care, elder care, flextime—but they were secondary issues except for small sectors of the population. The key issues were career development and contribution. People generally felt they were being under-utilized.

Changing Management Style

What have we done? We have invested considerable time in management and supervisory training. We are trying to change the style of management—from control-oriented to leadership-oriented. Leadership is empowering people, motivating people to take risks, encouraging employees to speak up, and sharing decision-making. We have said that in the future we will select managers who have leadership competencies.

We also redesigned our appraisal system. For the first time, managers are evaluated on their ability to manage as well as on their results. Now we encourage supervisors to talk about their employees' career development. We also introduced child and elder care services, a spouse employment assistance program, and expanded our EAP program. We issued a Mobil relationships statement that spelled out our beliefs. And we have focused on developing hub locations.

We believe the company culture has to change. In addressing the issues of leadership, flexibility and adap-

tability, we encourage all managers to work on the tough diversity issues, including those of individual family problems.

Harris Sussman
Senior Consultant
WorkWays

People have been living complicated lives for a long time. We are just beginning to scratch the surface of how big this issue is. We seldom admit how big an issue work-family is. Essentially we are trying to build a different world filled with humanity and hope and a different sense of human capacity.

Here is a sketch of this world. For the first time in U.S. history, the average married couple has more parents than children. The biggest issue of the U.S. workforce in the 1990s will be the death of our parents. We will be a workforce in mourning. The greatest challenge in human resources will be the ability to provide grief counseling and recovery. We haven't begun to tap into this. This isn't to mention the death of people from AIDS, which has just begun to affect us.

For the first time in U.S. history, there is no replacement workforce for the present workforce. In absolute numbers, there aren't enough people to replace us tomorrow. Given the school dropout rate, there are grave concerns about the readiness of young people to do the work we have been preparing for them. Each year 700,000 students don't graduate from high school and another 700,000 who do graduate can't read or write. Over 90 percent of the workforce in the year 2001 is already in the workforce. The big question is, How productive will we be and what do we know about the conditions required in order to be productive? Most people work at about 30-40 percent of their capacity. People don't bring the full range of themselves to work.

Work and Family as a Movement

What is work-family really about? In less than 20 years, we have created a body of knowledge and practice that didn't exist before. Work-family is a code, a euphemism, a metaphor for a movement for major social change. We don't often discuss it in these terms. All roads lead to work-family whether you come at it from EEO, policy, compensation, wellness programs, community relations, legislative compliance issues, benefits, or employee relations.

Work-family is the environment for productivity in the U.S., not a side issue to be put on a back burner. We are constructing a new social order. We are negotiating and redrawing the terms under which we will do work in our lives. Companies make social policy by omission or commission. We have not always recognized the ramifications of this. At the same time, companies function within a larger world so they should not be surprised that the work-family movement draws inspiration and concrete lessons from other movements of social change, including the civil rights movement, the women's movement and the environmental movement. These are integral underpinnings.

It used to be taboo to discuss personal things at work. Home was the place for personal life. This rule no longer applies. Work is not a separate country.

The single best thing our society can do to improve the future workplace is to provide prenatal care. Prenatal care needs to be high on the agenda of anyone dealing with human resource planning. It has taken business a long time to realize it should be involved in K-12 education; the Business Roundtable and Business Council have agreed to cooperate with the governors and the President in making education a priority.

Work and Family Frontiers

The next frontier for work-family is understanding more about the conditions under which people work best. Managers know little about making a work environment a learning environment—in which people can learn, grow and change. Most managers have given no thought about the conditions people require. Many years of work have already been done, but we must see work-family as the beginning of a new interdisciplinary field that cuts across every other function.

The basic assumptions of most organizational life are based on men's experiences. If you see a corporation in which few women are in high levels, you should ask about the nature of the corporation. Is there something in the inherent nature of American businesses that is inimical to women achieving success? Most companies don't think about how biased and arbitrary their policies and procedures are and how they are based on erroneous assumptions.

The key questions are:

- What are your models of change?
- What do you believe about human nature and its improvability?
- What is your experience with significant change in life, and do you think it is possible?
- What do you know about coaching people through a transformative process?

We are taking part in a historic movement to negotiate the terms of a new society, and we need all the anthropology and organizational ecology we can bring to bear on this task.

Government Efforts: Carrots Or Sticks For Business

Dallas L. Salisbury
President
Employee Benefit Research Institute

We have just tabulated the results of a survey of benefit professionals and government policy makers on what they viewed as the likely trends in economic security programs and employee benefits between now and 2000. Two trends easily ranked at top and were viewed not only as changes that will occur but also should occur.

Polls: Choice vs. Paternalism

First is the notion that by 2000, paternalism will be dead as a value among corporations and as a value in employment. And along with this, employees will exercise choice. People will begin to define the compensation package they prefer within given limitations. This is where the future is headed.

It is an interesting juxtaposition in a time of debates centering on Pepper Commission proposals for mandates in health insurance, and for state actions and mandates in health insurance, child care and parental leave. In surveys of members of Congress, congressional staff, and the private sector, a uniform message emerges that paternalism is bad and choice is good.

A recent EBRI/Gallup survey looked at individual attitudes toward health care. Of the surveyed population in a national random sample, 54 percent said government should provide all people access to health care. When asked how much they were willing to pay to get this from the government, the average response was $600 a year. Only 2 percent were willing to pay as much money as the program would actually cost. Even taxing the wealthiest 2 percent would not provide the $89 billion cost of the Pepper Commission proposals.

Polls: Choice vs. Mandates

Looking at employer mandates, 82 percent of the survey group said they wanted employers mandated to offer health insurance. Yet, when asked if given the choice—under a mandate—to receive an additional $1,500 in taxable compensation or health insurance, 54 percent said they would take the compensation. Their view of the mandate, when one surveys further, isn't that they are mandated to take it, but that somebody is mandated to offer it.

If we look at the same trend surveys, we find favorable views toward cafeteria plans, corporate and government focus on parental leave, referral services, on-site day care—particularly emergency on-site day care—and other child care and elder care options.

We asked a national random sample about their views on child care and parental leave issues, designing it so they could consider some of the state initiatives as well as the federal policy debate. These are key survey findings:

- 53 percent think that employers, rather than government, should be the primary players in dealing with family issues.
- 71 percent think that employers should show an interest in and promote flexibility; 67 percent felt the government had a role.
- 60 percent preferred on-site child care on an emergency basis; 26 percent preferred financial assistance; 12 percent opted for information and referral services.
- 62 percent favored employer involvement.

In follow-up questions, however, respondents say that employer involvement should provide options and mechanisms, not dictate how it will be sorted out. As for parental leave, 81 percent feel that employers should be required to allow individuals to take time without pay to care for their families. There seems to be some understanding of the difficulties that parental leave causes a company, but there is still a desire for choice and flexibility.

In the mandate debate, we frequently end up focusing on the issue of whether it is right for the government to tell people what to do. Our surveys indicate individuals want a mandate but they don't want to lose choice. They want government to force others to give them choice.

Mary Wendy Roberts
Commissioner of Labor
Bureau of Labor and Industries
State of Oregon

Oregon believes in choice and in parental leave. There has been great interest in developing policies and passing such legislation. I would like to see a more holistic approach but, as a politician and a pragmatist, I realize that we must fall back on incremental responses even though they sometimes create problems later on.

In Oregon we started with parental leave as the first part of an approach to family leave. Government has a legitimate role in this area. Mandates have a legitimate place, are inevitable, are necessary. When they are put in place, they work in many ways. They work in the sense that they respond to public concerns and needs. This is what government is about—to recognize what public concerns are, the social policies that are necessary as well as what is good for the economy.

Public Favors Family Leave Law

It is obvious that the public is interested in this subject. One national poll reported that four out of five registered voters said they favored a family leave bill that would provide 10 weeks of unpaid leave to new parents, adoptive parents, and for the care of sick children. Among these voters, the ratio is five to one for those who would be less favorable to a member of Congress who opposed such a bill. This legislation is inevitable. If the private sector had been able to implement this kind of leave, government wouldn't be playing a role. It did not happen, so here we are.

The debate on whether mandates should develop or not is past. We are already in the midst of them. Eight states have adopted legislation that affects new parents in the private sector. Oregon's 1987 law passed the house by 50 votes to 8 and the senate 22 to 6.

Oregon's Law

The law covers all employers in Oregon with 25 or more employees part-or full-time. The leave is 12 weeks and can be taken by one parent at a time. It may be split between the parents. Public employees are also covered. This covers just over 10 percent of the private employers in Oregon and represents 7,000 employers. When you consider the number of employees covered in the private sector, it is about 65 percent of the workforce.

Companies with cafeteria plans are exempt. We believe in flexibility and want to promote creative efforts by companies. An employee must give 30 days written notice before taking leave unless specified circumstances make this impossible. The leave is unpaid, but the employee may use accrued, paid vacation leave, sick leave, or other personal compensatory leave. Thus, more employees can afford to take the leave. In our initial surveys, we found that most employees who had taken leave—about one percent of the potential employees covered—utilized some form of paid leave during the time off.

Following expiration of the leave, the employee must be restored to her or his former position, or if that job has been eliminated for legitimate business reasons, an equivalent position. If this is not possible, they have to use an available and suitable position—one with comparable duties and pay at the same or nearby work site. There is no loss of seniority, vacation, sick leave, or other accrued benefits. Benefits do not accrue during the unpaid leave.

The Law's Success

The law is working. Since it went into effect, we have had a number of complaints—usually focused on the failure of management to allow an employee to use the paid sick leave they have accumulated. But the number of complaints have been small. Not a single company has said that they cut benefits because of this law or contemplated reducing benefits in other areas. This is a myth—that other benefits will be cut. Nearly all companies reported that there were no significant problems in adjusting to the law.

Subsequently, there has been a Ford Foundation study and survey. The very early results show that the formal, scientific study confirms the findings of our earlier surveys. There has not been any reduction in benefits. In fact, 88 percent of the employers surveyed said that implementation was not difficult; 27.4 percent said that it was extremely easy.

When we talk about the carrot and stick, we must recognize that many of the carrots are already in the marketplace if an employer has the vision to see them. Government's role is to provide encouragement—sometimes in the form of a mandate—which is not a reflection on the great work many corporations have done. Laws are not passed to change the behavior of the best corporate citizens but that of the worst corporate citizens. Government has a stake in it. I am proud of what we have done in Oregon.

Judith L. Lichtman
President
Women's Legal Defense Fund

The Family and Medical Leave Act, (FMLA) ready for floor action in Congress, offers job security but not income security because it provides an unpaid leave. I am embarrassed to be advocating an unpaid leave, but I do so because of economic and political realities. A large coalition of over 160 organizations has come to support job security, a very important provision for women and men who work and have family responsibilities.

FMLA: A National Family and Medical Leave Act

FMLA has two major parts: a medical leave of up to 15 weeks a year (13 weeks in the Senate version) pregnancy, child birth, and related medical conditions; and a separate family leave of 10 weeks that can be used within a two-year period for the birth, adoption, and serious illness of a child or parent of an employee. In the House, the bill covers employers with 50 or more employees and after three years, phases down to 35 or more employees. In the Senate, the bill provides coverage for employers with 20 or more employees. The leaves are unpaid, guarantee the same or equivalent job and the continuation of health insurance.

There are many state FMLAs: 25 states and Puerto Rico have some protection for some form of family and medical leave. They are often gender neutral, men or women may take the leave. The trend is toward gender-neutral family and medical leave. None of the states has paid leave.

FMLA: State Options

These are options promulgated in various states:
• Four states have family and medical leave laws—Connecticut, Maine, Wisconsin and Pennsylvania.
• Fours states have family leave but not medical leave laws—New Jersey, North Dakota, Oklahoma and West Virginia. All are for state employees only, except New Jersey.
• Four states have parental leave laws to care for newborns, newly adopted or seriously ill children—Minnesota, Oregon, Rhode Island and Washington.
• Twelve states and Puerto Rico have pregnancy

disability leave or "mommies only" laws—California, Florida, Hawaii, Iowa, Kansas, Louisiana, Massachusetts, Montana, New Hampshire, North Carolina, Tennessee and Vermont.
• Kentucky has an adoption leave law.

FMLA: Costs

Why is it important for the U.S. to have family and medical leave? The benefits of the policy far outweigh the costs. Today it costs society hundreds of millions of dollars a year because we don't have a policy guaranteeing people their jobs after a medical or family leave. The annual loss to working women and their families has been estimated at over $600 million. The annual loss to taxpayers from unemployment insurance and other government benefit programs is estimated to be over $100 million. These aggregate costs have a human dimension too.

The costs to business of implementing FMLA, on the other hand, would be low. The GAO estimates that the House of Representatives version of the bill will cost employers only $188 million a year, or $5.50 per covered worker. This figure is less than one-third of what it now costs workers *not* to have the leave. In addition minimum standard of family and medical leave will help American business compete for a better workforce.

A national minimum standard is necessary to guarantee family and medical leave for *all* employees. Without such a standard, not all businesses will provide the leave voluntarily. For some companies, the short-term hassle will appear to outweigh the long-term gain of workforce productivity and loyalty. We don't rely on companies to voluntarily pay the minimum wage, overtime or to refrain from exploiting children. For these important social values, we have a minimum labor standard. Accommodation for family caretaking ought to be in this same category.

If companies were providing family and medical leave voluntarily, we would expect an increase in such benefits in recent years. However, the most recent Bureau of Labor Statistics study shows that the incidence of job-guaranteed leave for birth has remained steady at about 33 percent over the past several years. The family and medical leave standard is both gender neutral and age neutral and thus discourages discrimination against women or parents with young children. Since people of all ages may take the leave, it doesn't pit one group of workers against another. And because the leave is available not just for birth and adoption but for serious illness of family members, the family and medical leave responds to the ongoing needs of employees who have children or other family responsibilities throughout their work lives.

The bill obviously helps working people and their families but, more important, it is a proposal to rebuild America not only by supporting American families but also by helping America be the best nation it can be. Smart employers want to accommodate the needs of working families because it means attracting and retaining experienced, trained, dedicated and hard working employees who will continue to make contributions to their companies.

James D. Burge
Corporate Vice President and Motorola Director of Government Affairs-Personnel
Motorola, Inc.

There are many thoroughbred companies addressing work-family issues today because it is a prudent, competitive, rational business decision. Most businesses face fierce competition in the global marketplace. Most of us fight for a fraction of a percent improvement in our margins just to survive to invest in tomorrow's technology or to invest in R&D that will create the jobs for tomorrow.

At Motorola, our total customer satisfaction program earned us the first Malcolm Baldrige Quality Award. We spread this quality message among our customers, our suppliers and our employees. This has moved us toward our goal of six sigma quality in the next few years. Six sigma means near perfect quality. It can be achieved only through a staff of competent, well trained, quality people. Quality people will produce quality products. Enlightened, thoroughbred companies are leading the way to eliminate or reduce work-family conflicts to attract, motivate and retain the quality workforce it needs to compete.

Mandates: Competitiveness and Choice Issues

The wage and benefit pot is finite. Business can expend only so much for total labor costs and remain competitive in the global marketplace. As mandates are considered, there is an associated cost with them. I must raise the question of whether this cost places the U.S. at a competitive disadvantage as we address the labor cost issue.

I am also concerned about mandates limiting choice. Motorola has been a strong advocate of dealing with our employees on the terms and conditions of employment that best suit their needs. If you accept the idea of the finite wage and benefit pot, the more mandates you put in place the fewer choices and options you can afford in dealing with employees. At Motorola we think that good benefit management is providing the greatest

benefit per dollar cost for the most employees.

Work-Family: Cost Effectiveness Issues

While we see demographics changing and know that we must address the work-family issue, it is not a very cost-effective program as far as benefit management is concerned. In our dependent care account, for example, only 700 of our 60,000 U.S. employees choose to participate in this tax-advantaged program. With parental and illness leave, we grant up to 13 weeks for illness, maternity, adoption or illness of parents—and this is job-guaranteed. Of 60,000 employees, only 147 are participating in the maternity leave program. In our resource and referral program, we received 180 inquiries per month at first; this declined to 50 per month; and now it has leveled off to 40 per month. Even with this low participation, we think it is a prudent business decision to address work-family with these programs.

Management: Diversity Issues

We are working hard to help our female workers break through the glass ceiling with mentors, role models and networking. We are accelerating the gestation period for women and minorities moving through our management programs. We have done a good job of filling the pipeline in the bottom half. Now we must work to move people through the middle and upper management ranks.

Flexibility is the buzzword in our supervisory training for managing work and family issues. We have created a number of cottage industries with computers in the home as well as using flexible hours, part-time jobs and job sharing. At Motorola it is okay to be a mom or dad first. We are also sensitive to the dual-career relocation issue. We make sure that we don't create a dead-end career path for an individual simply because he or she has turned down a move because of a spouse's job. Career tracks at different stages and different ages are okay. Our employee assistance plan provides counseling in various areas of work and family. It is only those companies that voluntarily step up to these issues that will be able to attract and retain the competent employees they will need in the global future.

We are all addressing the issue of moving from EEO compliance to managing workforce diversity. In 1950, 33 percent of women were in the workforce; now this number is moving toward 80 percent. With our investments in training, there is no way we want to lose qualified workers who can manufacture products that are on the leading edge of technology. There is no way we want to lose a quality workforce because of work and family conflict.

The Cost-Benefits of a "Family-Friendly" Workplace

James J. Renier
Chairman and Chief Executive Officer
Honeywell Inc.

Business needs specific, targeted work-family programs because they will help alleviate immediate problems faced by our employees and their families. The roots of these problems lie deep in the home and business infrastructure. The permanent solution must heal the cleavage that today divides work and the family. If there is any kind of permanent solution here, it will involve restructuring work/family relations around our core values.

Work vs. Family

We are all more productive when we can give work and home their due time. This is becoming increasingly harder to manage. What time we have is often of a lesser quality. Today our jobs assume a far greater importance in our lives than ever before. Most people identify themselves closely with their jobs and with the personal rewards work brings them.

Workers with families are torn by competing forces because their family responsibilities are also demanding. Company culture traditionally tells them to leave their family troubles at home. This is frequently impossible today because there is seldom anyone at home.

I would ask how you spend your time, and where your interests lie. We must ask ourselves if we are delegating work or delegating our children. We must all examine our consciences about this.

Families in Crisis

Family crises are rapidly increasing as the traditional family structure breaks apart. Single parents are common and mothers are rushing back to work to augment family income. In 1960 over one-third of women had jobs; by 2000 it will be close to two-thirds. During the past two decades, the fastest growing segment of the labor force has been married women with young children. More than half the mothers of children under one-year-old now work outside the home; 57 percent of mothers of children under six have jobs. By 1995 two-thirds of all preschool children and three-fourths of school-aged children will have mothers in the workforce. This represents a huge societal change. I am not, however, advocating a return to the past.

Business and Education in Crisis

Today we need educated American mothers and fathers to maintain a competitive workforce. Tomorrow we will need their children. Projections aren't reassuring. The growth of the workforce has been slowing. And the forecast is that by 2000 as many as 23 million jobs may go unfilled due to educational deficiencies. Industry now spends millions annually to train and retrain employees. But the effectiveness of training and education in general depends largely on the quality of early learning. We need people who are not only verbally and mathematically literate but who also have analytical ability and disciplined work habits. They must also be able to learn quickly. Today the median education required in industry is 12.8 years; 10 years from now it will be 13.5 years. The hurdles are all getting higher.

About one-fourth of American youth drop out of school. We lose one million graduates a year; almost a million who do graduate are functionally illiterate. It is calculated that those who drop out each year cost this country $240 billion over the course of their lifetimes in lost wages and taxes. An international study showed that American 14-year-olds ranked 14th out of 17 countries in basic science knowledge. In math, American 13-year-olds placed last. We can't return to our former productivity as long as educational requirements rise and achievement decline. Without an educated workforce, business cannot compete.

Children at Risk

The problems are usually blamed on the schools. But often parents have not done their jobs. We must look at ourselves and do our part to send kids to school ready to learn. This is much tougher when parents are not home. Most of our underachieving children are poor and, for them, we know that early intervention can be helpful. We need to see that their mothers receive prenatal care and training. We must also see that newborns receive care and that their nutritional needs are met. We must insure that children have the basics so that they are ready to learn when they reach kindergarten.

Then there are the children who are not poor but whose parents work full time and are too busy—stretched by the tension between work and home. Children at risk don't just live in inner cities; they also live in wealthy suburbs. These, too, are children at risk. Without a family structure that provides attention, guidance and nurturing, children are deprived of the early preparation that promises later success. With family structure diminished, a child's first source of empowerment is gone; the child is not ready for the second source of empowerment—the school.

The Value of Early Education

Is this situation hopeless? No, but it requires significant changes in thinking. My company has traditionally made education an important part of our funding activity. Since the 1960s, we have worked closely with educators to make life in the business world real to both students and teachers. Our support has been aimed at the college level because we recruit many technical and professional graduates. But it has become clear that the colleges cannot help children who are not well prepared in earlier grades. We now realize that we must target children as early as the prenatal stage.

I testified recently on this subject before the House Committee on Education and Labor. I asserted that business people are convinced that if we fail to nurture and educate all our children, we will close the doors of the future to growing numbers of young people. The cost of the failure will be enormous. The stakes are nothing less than the survival of the free enterprise economy, our democratic system and the American dream.

It is encouraging that the National Governors' As-

sociation endorsed President Bush's education program—with its specific objectives that all disadvantaged children have access to high quality preschool programs and receive good nutrition and health care. The value of early intervention in the educational process has been amply documented in research over the years. On this issue, business must take a long-term approach. We must look years ahead and we will probably sacrifice some short-term results.

The Corporate Agenda

What can business do? We can analyze problems, identify needs, propose solutions, muster resources, organize support, develop strategies, execute plans, evaluate results and help the public sector reinstitutionalize a system that takes all the new family norms into account.

A good example is a program we developed in Minneapolis. In 1988 I noted in my activities in the United Way that a growing number of groups were interested in the promise of early childhood education. Those interested included the mayor's office, business people, the Community Development Alliance, the Minneapolis Day Care Association, the Minneapolis Citizens' League and so on. I chaired a task force that decided early on that community collaboration was part of the answer.

We named our initiative Success by Six, with the conviction that children who are prepared for kindergarten have a good start on successful lives. Success by Six focused on the things we could accomplish best as a coordinating leadership group:

(1) Develop a community consensus on the best strategic approaches to eliminate barriers. Our role wasn't to replace public sector or private initiatives. Our role was to knock down barriers so these two sectors could work better.

(2) Build a community-wide commitment to coordinate action.

(3) Maintain a large, accurate information base for the use of interested organizations.

(4) Provide funding in support of pilot efforts. We now have a prenatal program underway in a poor urban neighborhood. And at Honeywell corporate headquarters, we plan to open a school for pregnant teenagers to help out the local school system.

Community groups are coming together to attack problems cooperatively. The Dayton-Hudson Corporation has tackled one of the most difficult jobs—alerting everyone in the Twin-Cities area that there is a crisis. Presentations have been made to Minnesota's U.S. senators, representatives and governor, to the leaders of the state legislature and to appropriate committees. The Minneapolis Chamber of Commerce and the Minnesota

Business Partnership, made up of seas of 200 Minnesota companies, have added early childhood to their agendas. We are stimulating the efforts of Minnesota companies, social organizations, government departments, business associations and the media. Most important, we have strengthened the cooperation between business, government and civic groups. Initiating this collaboration may be the most valuable contribution a company can make.

Core Value

I am confident about the future. American industry still leads the world. Today Japan has an economy of $2.8 trillion; America's is $5.2 trillion. We are still exporting more technology than we import. But the contest is finding the best solution to the work-family relationship. We must return to a core of values.

Many things human resources wants to do are difficult because the average business person doesn't see where they fit in the framework of the whole problem. If the business community is convinced that early childhood education must be resurrected in this country, industry will support whatever is needed to get there—including day care and other family supportive measures.

No business person believes that we can succeed long-term without educated children. Business badly needs the creative thinking that these programs can trigger. We must remember that the old solutions won't work. We must restructure our national educational system to insure that all children get early education. And we must work diligently to force effective community action. The future of American business and the American family depends on it.

The Conference Board
845 Third Avenue
New York, N.Y. 10022

Nonprofit Org.
U.S. Postage
PAID
Baltimore, MD
Permit No. 5280

The Conference Board

Supplement to "Work and Family Policies: The New Strategic Plan" *R-949*

The Globalization of Work-Family Policies

Recognizing a need and responsibility to its employees and communities, Du Pont is working hard to blend the needs of children and their families into its corporate agenda around the world.

Here are human resources managers from Du Pont to discuss:

- *Family-friendly alternatives from France, England, and Sweden*
- *Canada's chronic shortage of high quality, affordable child care facilities*
- *Germany's and Japan's aging population*

Faith A. Wohl
Director, Work Force Partnering
The Du Pont Company

I want to broaden and deepen the discussion of work-family issues to acknowledge the real significance of what we are doing as we discuss new ways to integrate work and family. Whether we put it on the table or not, we are working on an issue whose solution will help determine the quality of life—in fact the kind of world—our children and grandchildren will inherit.

I am a work and family advocate within the corporate community. I have been on this mission at Du Pont for five years. I have been a "living subject" for almost 30 years—as a working mother and grandmother.

In these years I have learned how to talk about work and family: to present it as a productivity boost, to define its cost-benefit dimensions, to be ready to demonstrate how successful work and family solutions can be in doing everything from building morale to reducing absenteeism.

Children Not Province of U.S. Managers

"Children seem so unbusiness-like." They seem to be the province of someone else. So in the business world, we focus on our employees who are, after all, our appropriate concern and greatest asset. It is for them we build child care centers, contract with referral services, extend our focus to elder care, design flexible work practices and so on. In five years, I have used that language well.

I did this because it is clear that unless companies produce toys or video programs or breakfast cereals, they just don't think about kids. Fundamentally they are seen as someone else's responsibility. This was clear to me until last March when I visited France as part of an American study team—sent by the French American Foundation—to study the French child care system, one of the best in the world.

There I met business people who think about children in a remarkable way. When our business community thinks about child care, it sees children as one more problem to be managed so we can assure ourselves of a work force that is on the job, on time, everyday. In France, in contrast, one thing became very clear: children are a resource to be cherished. The French see child care as an investment, not a cost, as a long-term societal commitment supported by broad agreement in every sector. As one French employer said, "We are not accountants when it comes to children."

Since then I have done research and learned that many other countries shape their government and work policies around what is good for children. This is very different from American pragmatism that puts the needs of the workplace first. By saying this, I don't suggest that we don't love our own children. I am saying that we don't share a concern for each other's children in the way it seems to happen in other places. Unless you understand that a different frame of reference may be operating in a given country, their policies may make no economic sense to you.

Shaping Government & Work Policies Around Children

In England, for example, 40 weeks of partially paid leave are provided to new mothers. The English share a belief that children must get a good start and that mothers and babies need to be together. In Sweden, large numbers of mothers and fathers work six-hour days—a schedule guaranteed by law to parents until their children are eight years old. This is in a country that also says children have the right to a place in a quality day care center. In France, children ages three to six may use a free, universally available, high quality preschool system that offers full-day programs; 97 percent of the eligible children use the programs, whether their parents work or not.

I have become very interested in global work and family practices. I see them as a possible source for what we might do at Du Pont. Our company is increasingly global: In a few years, more than half our earnings will come from outside the U.S.; we have facilities in 60 countries on six continents; we have 140,000 employees all over the globe. If I can gain a new frame of reference for work and family issues here in the U.S., I will better understand how a global company might respond to the needs of its employees, its communities and its future. In America we must insert the needs of children and their families into our strategic plan.

With me today are human resource managers from Du Pont—from Germany, Canada and Japan—who will serve as windows for us to look through to see how work-family issues are playing out in their countries.

Andrea Englert-Rygus
Personnel Manager
Du Pont Canada, Inc.

Child care: In Canada, the minimum legislated standard is a 17-week unpaid maternity leave with a guarantee of the same wages in the same/comparable position upon return to the employer. Women must meet certain employment criteria to qualify for this leave. Many provinces and businesses have augmented this minimum requirement. Although women aren't earning income while on leave, they can apply for unemployment insurance benefits for 15 weeks coverage. This allowance is paid from a federal fund into which all workers and employers in Canada must contribute. This benefit is taxable income. There are currently a number of government initiatives under review for extending/broadening the whole arena of leaves and applicable benefits. We also have a "baby bonus" or children's allowance of $33.33 per month per child. This may/may not be taxable based on income level.

Supplementing the Informal Network

We are facing a chronic shortage of high quality, affordable child care facilities, particularly infant care. Many parents in Canada rely on the informal network—the neighbor, the grandmother, unlicensed day care. Some people use day care centers or nannies if they can find and afford them.

The government provides a child care tax credit up to a maximum of $4,000 a year per child, given that certain requirements are fulfilled, perhaps most importantly having receipts. For parents using the informal network, the caregiver is normally paid under the table and receipts are not provided. Parents who use licensed day care centers, nannies or caregivers where receipts are provided can use the tax credit, but it still doesn't begin to cover the amount actually spent during the year. Some Canadian companies—usually the larger firms—provide child care support. The most common supports are expansion of the basic maternity leave legislation or resource and referral services.

Elder care: This is a growing issue for us and was illustrated at Du Pont Canada last year in our work and family study where a large number of employees told us they are now part of the "sandwich generation." Not only are they struggling as working parents to raise children but they are also coping with aging or ailing parents. We are now trying to focus on elder care as well as child care.

Hans E. Goedden
Director, Employee Relations,
Du Pont De Nemours (Deutschland) G.M.B.H.

Child care: Family is a strong traditional value in Europe. In Germany, government, community institutions, churches and business are complementary in their efforts to solve child care issues. Legislation provides the following: paid maternity leave from six weeks before birth to eight weeks after; children's assistance for all mothers—not only those

employed—for 12 months in the amount of 900 DM per month; parental leave up to 12 months after birth; child care leave if the mother must care for the child during office hours; and other benefits.

Parents have tax-deductibles during the period they are raising children. Community child care facilities are maintained through taxes; by churches through the church tax (9 percent of income tax goes to the churches); by private welfare institutions; and by businesses in an increasing number. The total number of child care facilities is about 1.5 million, with 3.5 million children in the eligible category.

German Policies Change with Demographics

Elder care: Germany has an aging population. We also have the lowest birth rate in Europe, if not the world, about 0.9 percent. This means that the percentage of people age 60 and older will increase from 20.6 percent in 1987 to over 37 percent in the year 2040. Government has increased the retirement age to 65. Sickness insurance has been extended to cope with the cost of elder care. Tax concessions for elder caregivers are being established. We need fewer hospitals so now they are being converted to elder homes. And at-home services for elders are being developed. Business realizes that this is a growing market and is developing meals-on-wheels, hygienic or medical in-house care, and building retirement housing.

Workplace flexibility: Germany pioneered flextime about 15-20 years ago. The principle is that you define for your work force a core working time when everyone must be present. Normally this is between 9 a.m. and 3:30 p.m. You then establish a time frame within which everyone may choose when they want to begin or end work. An interesting aspect is that at the end of the month, you establish a credit or debit opposite the contractual working time, which is still 40 hours a week. This credit can be converted to half or full days off, up to a limit, such as two half-days or one full day a month.

Job sharing has also grown since its first introduction into industry. Job sharing exists when two or more employees share one or more jobs. The schedule is determined by the participating employees, again, within the required contractual working time for the position.

Toshimitsu Yamaguchi,
Employee Relations Specialist,
Du Pont Japan

Child care: The Japanese family highly values child caring. Responsibility for care tends to fall to the female. After university graduation, women come to the labor market for about four to six years. After marriage and giving birth, they leave the company and devote themselves to child care. About 10 years later, they return to the work force on a part-time basis. They return part-time due to the long commuting time in Japan—the average commute is three hours round trip—and the lack of shared child care among Japanese couples. In addition, only 19 percent of Japanese companies have implemented child care leave. Public child care centers are rigid—opening from 9 a.m. to 4:30 p.m. only. It is very difficult for working women with babies. They tend to depend on their mothers or their grandmothers.

Elder care: This is a key issue in Japan. Our life span is number one in the world—81 years for females and 75 years for males. In 1988 the ratio of those 65 and older to the total population was 11 percent; in 2025, it will be over 23 percent, the largest such ratio in the world. It will take Japan only 25 years to reach this ratio; the U.S., 70 years; France, 130 years.

Japan's Family Structure Goes Nuclear

Traditionally, the Japanese family was very large, including three to four generations; now 80 percent of the families are nuclear. This trend began in 1950. Company-supported programs are poor. Only 13 percent of our companies have initiated a three-month unpaid elder care leave policy. Governmental support is critical and lacking. We have much to do here.

Workplace flexibility: Flexible work practices are limited to directors of companies—especially in R&D—and software and information systems engineers. Some companies are adopting a core time, from 10 a.m. to 3 p.m., when employees must be present. We are still in the experimental stage with this issue.

The Conference Board, 845 Third Avenue, New York, New York 10022
The Conference Board Europe, Avenue Louise, 207 - Bte 5, B-1050 Brussels, Belgium
The Conference Board of Canada, 255 Smyth Road, Ottawa, Ontario, KIH-8M7